White Flag

Stories about God and us and how the freedom
we want looks a lot like surrender

Unless otherwise stated, all scriptures are taken from the New International Version.

Cover design by Hawk Design at
www.hawkdesign.graphics

First Printing: 2015

ISBN 978-0692523292

ROCKET FARMER

matt@rocketfarmer.net
1870 W 2700 S
Syracuse, Utah 84075

To learn more about the author and to order additional copies of this book visit
www.mattjones.ca

White Flag

Stories about God and us and how the freedom
we want looks a lot like surrender

by

Matthew Jones

First Edition: Published 2015

For my church.

It is a joy being your pastor.

Table of Contents

How to read this book...

A number of years ago, I became convinced that God's Word had a lot more for me than I was getting out of it, and that the problem wasn't the quality of the commentaries I was using. Rather, it was that the Bible had become a textbook for me.

As a pastor, I think I can speak for many of my peers when I say that it can be easy to allow our study time in preparation for teaching to take the place of personal time with God's Word where we just allow Him to speak to us.

In order to combat this problem, a few years ago I figured out a simple system that helped me to form a habit of reading God's Word personally each day. The system has 3 parts to it. I **reflect** on my day (what I've done and how I've felt), I **read** God's Word (one chapter), I **respond** to it (in a journal), and then I approach God's throne boldly with a **request** (a prayer that is both spoken and written). This system is explained in a bit more detail at the end of the book in the section called **Your Turn**.

With that in mind, let me be clear that this book is a companion piece. It won't make much sense without also reading God's Word (the Bible) with each chapter.

This book is the product of a personal 50-day journey through the book of Genesis. Each day I would read a chapter from Genesis, meditate on it and then respond to it with my own writing. I want to encourage you to use this as a daily devotional of sorts for your own journey through Genesis over the next 50 days. Read one chapter in Genesis each day along with its corresponding chapter in this book. Then, I'd encourage you to respond and reflect on what you've read in some type of journal. Finally, finish your time by asking God directly for his power in some area of your life. The entire process should take less than 10 minutes.

If you'd rather consume it in larger chunks over fewer days, that's fine too. I did the same when I edited it and still felt I got a lot out of it. Just make sure that you read the scripture passage that goes with each chapter.

By the way, this is not a commentary. When I teach at my church, I often go verse-by-verse to get every ounce of truth out of each word. In my personal time with God, however, I tend to read God's Word more as narrative. These are stories that God inspired His prophets to write so that I could know Him better. It is with that intent, that I would encourage you to read this book. Each writing is an attempt to pull something life-changing and relevant out of what are often merely historical writings for people. To that end, this book is my attempt to prove that you don't have to just read a book like Psalms to find encouragement for your day. All scripture is profitable, as Paul said to Timothy, and I hope this book helps you in some small way to rediscover that.

My prayer is that this book would be a catalyst for you that draws you into God's Word for a few moments each day. I believe that if we will make that commitment, He'll show up and do the rest over time.

Thanks for reading, and I hope you enjoy it!

Matthew Jones

In the beginning...

No, not in the beginning of time, but rather the beginning of God's Word—God inspired the prophet Moses to record His message to His people. In all, Moses wrote 5 books—the first 5 books that appear in our Bible, otherwise known as the Torah. The first of these 5 books, Genesis, is the source material for the book you're now holding.

So why is Genesis so special? For some, its value lies in its explanation of the origins of our universe. For others, like the nation of Israel, it is the foundational document for their right to the promised land in Israel. For me however, it is not quite so lofty and far-reaching and is, in fact, intensely personal.

No other book in the Bible has as many stories about God interacting with man. The opening book of the Bible contains God's original stories about what life with Him actually looks like. Genesis is a collection of stories that together form a cohesive description of the type of relationship that God wants to have with us. Specifically, he wants to walk in fellowship with us as he did with Adam. He wants to walk in covenant with us as he did with Abraham. He also invites us to walk with him in faith as he did with Joseph. That last one is perhaps toughest as it requires you to trust him when his presence isn't evident—when things are going REALLY bad.

You will find that there is a central theme that rings true in this book, though it was not planned by me (Matt). That theme is **SURRENDER**. Over and over again, God's people are called to surrender to his will for their life, without knowing the future. When they were willing to take this step of faith, they found ultimate contentment with their purpose. When they strayed from it, they found only frustration.

Jesus would later express this foundational truth like this...

"Whoever wants to save their life will lose it, but whoever loses their life for me will find it."

Matthew 16:25

Isn't this what we all want? To truly **find** our life? To find our purpose or destiny or our part in this (insert your favorite journey metaphor here) and make peace with it? To let go of worrying about the future and just let God take the wheel?

With this theme as the backdrop, I want to invite you on a 50-day journey through the book of Genesis and I hope the writings in this book will be a tool to help you in your quest to get all you can out of it.

Now, let's begin in the beginning...

Genesis 1

I hate to start out like this, but I have to admit that whenever I read through Genesis 1 these days it seems to come with some real baggage. That's an awful feeling to have about God's Word, isn't it? I do, though. I seriously have negative emotions that come flooding into my mind from past experiences that I've had discussing the passage with others.

This part of the Bible has divided people, both inside the church (amongst ourselves) and outside of it. I personally know many people who find the idea of God simply unbelievable because of some of the claims that some people claim have been made in Genesis in general, and the opening chapter specifically.

It seems strange that a passage meant to explain God's design for perfect fellowship has been the source of so much division, doesn't it?

All of this seeks to rob me of the central message in Genesis 1— that I am the most special part of God's creation. In fact, I'm kind of the point of it all. The entire universe was made for God to tell one story...that **I was made in His image**! That's the source of understanding of who I am and why I'm here. I was made in the image of the one who made me. The "Imago Dei". The very image of God.

What is an image? Well, I suppose we all have some ideas and examples of what an image is. It's a visual representation of something, right? Perhaps a photograph. Perhaps millions of digital pixels. In the Bible though, this word is probably best defined as a **reflection**. To be made in the image of God means that something about Him is reflected in me.

What could it be? Is it His love? Is it his morality? If so, then why don't I measure up to Him in that regard? Instead of settling in on this idea that the image of God is something in our nature (how we are like him), I'd like to challenge you to consider that it's more a statement of God's purpose. God wants to reveal himself exclusively through mankind. Through you and me.

Let's me explain it this way...if you read Genesis 1 again, you should find a real sense of order to it. It is a poem of sorts that has six "verses" called "days" that all end with this simple refrain *"and there was evening and there was morning"*. What happens in those verses is also ordered accordingly. In the first couple of days, God creates water, sky and earth. He then proceeds to fill all three places with living things. He makes sea creatures for the water, birds for the sky and land animals for the earth. He also gives each the ability to reproduce **after its own kind**. Did you catch that? Every living thing is made to reproduce other creatures like itself. However, this purpose is somewhat different for man...

*"Then God said, 'Let us make man **in our image**, after our likeness. And let them have dominion over the fish of the sea and over the birds of the heavens and over the livestock and over all the earth and over every creeping thing that creeps on the earth.'*

*[27] So God created man **in his own image**, in **the image of God** he created him; male and female he created them.*

*[28] And God blessed them. And God said to them, '**Be fruitful and multiply** and fill the earth and subdue it, and have dominion over the fish of the sea and over the birds of the heavens and over every living thing that moves on the earth.'"*

Genesis 1:26-28

Let's recap for a second...God makes places for living things to live and then gives them the purpose of reproducing others in their own likeness. Then God makes man in his own image and gives them the same purpose—to reproduce **according to the likeness with which they were created**.

Simply put, our purpose is to multiply the likeness of God throughout the world. Wow. What an incredible task. So, if that is our purpose—to reflect God's likeness—then the natural question is "what is God like?"

The answer to that question, is found in God's Word and is the reason why we need to read it in the first place. God gave implicit instructions to reflect His image, and then gave us the rest of His Word to help us understand what it means to do that. His desire in giving us His Word is so that we can **know Him**.

That's what Genesis 1 is about. It's not God's attempt to explain particle physics to us. It's about how He centered all of creation around **you**. When all is said and done, God is setting the stage for the next 2 chapters, when he reveals what he truly wants: **a relationship with us**. That's why it's so important for those of us who know Him to reflect his image to the rest of the world— because he wants them to know Him too.

My prayer for you is that you are consumed by this one thought all day long: you bear the image of your Creator in a world that is in desperate need of Him. Make sure that you are learning how to show Him to the world.

Genesis 2

Since we've already established that everything was made for man and that he is the crown jewel of creation, we now arrive at chapter 2, where, after a brief description of how all life was formed from the ground up, God gives man another purpose on earth.

This is the kind of stuff that should fascinate us about God's Word. In Genesis 1, we are told that man was to "subdue" creation and have "dominion" over it. I'm sure we all have our own ideas of what that might look like, and I can imagine that many of them might not conjure up negative emotions. "Subduing" and "dominion" are terms that we perhaps equate with ancient kings and their tyranny over the people they rule. If we stop at Genesis 1, we might get the impression that God wants us to show plants and animals who's boss, and not give much thought about their part in our ecosystem.

However, Genesis chapter 2 paints a very different picture of man's relationship with creation. First, recognize that God makes a point in chapter 1 to say that plants and animals were here before man (which, by the way, science agrees with). Not only that, but here we are told that we were all formed from the same ground. I believe he does this to rightfully setup the next big "ah-

hah" moment. It may sound a little like "tree-hugger" stuff, so get
ready...

*"The Lord God took the man and put him in the garden of Eden
to work it and keep it."*

Genesis 2:15

Let's have a look at those words for a moment. First, the word
translated for "work" is the Hebrew word "abad". This word's
meaning is to work **for** something or better yet, to **serve**. In fact,
as you read the earlier portions of the chapter, you see that plants
and trees were designed to be in need of man's care...

*"...no small plant of the field had yet sprung up—for the Lord God
had not caused it to rain on the land, and there was no man to
work the ground."*

Genesis 2:5

Second, the word for "keep" is the Hebrew word "shamar" which
means to keep, watch or preserve. It is used elsewhere in the
Bible in reference to bodyguards, gatekeepers and watchmen.

No matter what side of the political aisle you are on, God's word
is clear in these few words that we are to serve and to protect our
planet with the utmost care. It also supports us by way of food,
oxygen, etc. Perhaps the best word to summarize God's intention
for the relationship between man and creation is harmony.

We are given another purpose at the end of the chapter in the creation of woman. Adam had noticed that other creatures were not alone, but until then, he had been. He put this longing best after God made a woman for him saying...

*"This **at last** is bone of my bones, and flesh of my flesh."*

Genesis 2:23

Notice the phrase "at last". It's as if Adam is saying "finally, my life is complete!"

While this goes on to specifically speak of marriage, if you keep it in the context of God's command to multiply in chapter 1, we realize here that we are to continue to grow as a human race and the best way to do that is to recognize that we are all human, as Adam did. That we were created equal, and that we need to live in relationship to each other, not just to procreate.

In summary, it is here we find 2 of the 3 great purposes for man: to live in harmony with creation and in fellowship with each other. Perhaps now the next time you bring flowers home to your wife, it will have much more meaning!

Genesis 3

God detests sin. Why? It destroys what is good. He created us so that He could enjoy us forever, but He made us in His likeness. This means that we understand that there is a difference between good and bad, and that line is not blurry. What we have here is the forces of evil trying to destroy what God created, and the start of a war that has been waged ever since.

What we must not miss here is the aftermath. What happened as a result of man's rebellion?

"Then the Lord God said, 'Look, the human beings have become like us, knowing both good and evil. What if they reach out, take fruit from the tree of life, and eat it? Then they will live forever!' So the Lord God banished them from the Garden of Eden..."

Genesis 3:22-23

Perhaps in your Bible this passage is titled "God's Judgment", and indeed, it is. However, we must understand God's reasoning for it. It's not just about punishment for sin. There is something much more eternal at stake. The state of creation before this moment was a universe without death. Everything was designed, as far as we know anyway, to endure. When God says "then they will live forever", He is not saying that he never intended that to happen. Of course God wants us to live forever and I believe he designed us to live eternally with him. He just doesn't want the people that we have become to live forever.

From the beginning we were designed not for evil things, but to do good works (Ephesians 2:10). Ever since Adam and Eve rebelled against God's commands each one of us has gone our own way and started living to please ourselves rather than our creator. God knows that this is a path that can only end in our ultimate destruction, so he separates, in a sense, our spiritual self from our physical self. This is seen in our removal from the Garden, and our inability on our own to re-enter it. By allowing us to die, our sins die in our bodies while our spirit can be saved and made new again.

Notice that immediately Adam and Eve recognize and are ashamed of their nakedness. It's like a picture of their failure to them and they can't imagine allowing God to see them like this, and so they try to cover themselves up with leaves, but God is not satisfied and has a better solution already in mind...

"And the Lord God made clothing from animal skins for Adam and his wife."

Genesis 3:21

I don't know if you caught that, but in that one verse lies the first hint of God's plan for salvation. Where did God get the animal skins from? From animals of course. Dead ones. How did they die? We must assume that God put them to death, and shed their blood to provide a covering for the sin of Adam and Eve. What a sad, beautiful picture.

You see, Genesis is all about **beginnings**. We have learned about the beginning of the universe, the beginning of man, the beginning of sin and now, the beginning of God's plan to put all of us broken people back together.

Celebrate this today—that the same God who we offended with our sin also made a way so that we could spend eternity with Him in spite of it.

Genesis 4

As you read the tragic story of Cain and Abel (and more notably that of Cain) you might be struck with the question of "where were their parents during all of this?"

Perhaps to be fair, we must remember that Adam and Eve had no parents themselves to teach them how to raise children, but on a more serious note, Eve's response to bearing children is very telling...

> *"Now Adam had sexual relations with his wife, Eve, and she became pregnant. When she gave birth to Cain, she said, 'With the Lord's help, I have produced a man!'"*
>
> Genesis 4:1

True, Eve did give some credit to the Lord...He is, after all, the creator of all things. But noticed how she uses that word "**produced**" in reference to Cain. In fact, Cain's name sounds very similar to a Hebrew word that means either to produce or to acquire. Both of these words carry with it the idea that "this is mine" or "I made this myself".

The chapter continues by giving us the broad strokes of the result of Cain's sin. What was Cain's sin anyway? Of course, hindsight being 20/20, perhaps we think that Cain's sin was that God requires the sacrifice of a lamb, not of crops. But of course, the law had yet to be given. Also, that would seem to make God look petty. One theme presented here that rings true throughout the Bible is this: God looks at the heart.

Cain presented some of his crops. Nothing special is mentioned. Apparently an opportunity for worship came up and perhaps he was taught to bring a gift to the Lord to symbolize this. Cain's thought process is "No biggie...I'll just grab some of the turnips I harvested yesterday and bring those."

Abel's sacrifice has much more meaning though. His thought process is "I've worked hard to raise this flock, but I wouldn't have any of them if not for God. Therefore I will pick my prized possession and give that to God as an expression of my gratitude."

Abel's offering more adequately expresses a heart that says "I know where all of this came from, and I want to say thanks."

Cain's focus is not just directed away from God, it is also directed toward something else entirely - **his work**. Does that sound like anyone else you know? Perhaps someone you saw this morning in some reflective surface?

The worst part is that Cain's mentality became generational. As the chapter continues to describe his descendants, we find that they are characterized by their **achievements** rather than their devotion to God.

Isn't it great however that we serve a God of second chances?

Eve is blessed in the end with a third child. This time, she doesn't mention producing or acquiring anything. Her attitude has changed and she names her son Seth. Do you know what Seth means? It means **granted**. Eve's attitude is, "I have been given this son by the Lord, not merely helped by Him to produce one."

This is the attitude we must have with everything we have been given. This is the attitude of true worship. It is this attitude that concludes our passage with these words...

"At that time people began to call upon the name of the Lord..."

Genesis 4:26

My prayer for myself, and for you the reader, is that all of us will experience such a time.

Genesis 5

While this is the first chapter in the Bible devoted entirely to genealogy, it will not be the last. The question is, if we're doing a chapter-per-day devotional, what can we really glean from this passage? At first glance, perhaps not much. However, if we reflect on both what happened before as well as after, we can arrive at least at one central theme: hope.

What we know from before is that a number of people were of Cain's descent. Based on our own experiences, we can probably assume that, like us, other generations from other lines also became so consumed with their own lives that they too forgot about their creator. It's not hard to understand how society would experience a simultaneous progression in cultural discovery (via the tools, music and cities of Cain's sons) and regression in morality by each one turning their hand to their own way (Isa. 53:6).

If Tolkien said it best that *"not all those who wander are lost"* then certainly the reverse of that is true as well. Perhaps many who have arrived really haven't. We may appear to be on the right track and getting better outwardly, but we're dying inside more every day.

You can be sure though, that some vestige of grace remained among a few of the people. Perhaps only from stories told to them as children, a small light of hope flickered in a few hearts of Adam's line. And you can be sure of this as well, that just as Cain and Seth were very intentionally named, so was the eventual incarnation of this hope in the person of Noah. We don't know exactly what hardship had befallen the people then, only that Noah's father Lamech said this about his son's birth...

"Out of the ground that the Lord has cursed, this one shall bring us relief from our work and from the painful toil of our hands."

Genesis 5:29

Notice that word 'relief'. In fact, the word could be best expressed as comfort or rest. The idea is that life was oppressive, perhaps monotonous, and very difficult and Noah's life would bring about a change to all of that.

I know it can be hard this side of the history to understand God's choice in the flood. We just can't possibly know the extent of the evil on the earth during that time. For all we know, it was as much God's mercy as it was his judgment that lead him to destroy mankind. What we do know is this, that God began a pattern here of using those who still call upon His name as the catalyst to bring about great change. We understand this—that the challenge so eloquently paraphrased by Mahatma Gandhi is subtly calling to us in the pages of God's word from ancient days before: "Be the change you want to see in the world."

Genesis 6

Sometimes I read a verse that just challenges me. Typically when this happens, I am forced to be blind of the forest on account of all the trees, or rather I miss the larger point of a passage because of my inability to get over one line. Genesis 6 provides just such a verse...

"And the Lord regretted that he had made man on the earth, and it grieved him to his heart."

Genesis 6:6

See what I mean? I read that and just can't get off it. Pity too, as the story of Noah is full of symbolism and great narrative. It speaks of the importance of marriage in God's divine plan and contains the forerunner to Isaiah 53:6 in verse 12 with the line *"all flesh had corrupted their way on the earth."*

Yet, anytime I read chapter 6, none of that matters. Why? Because I can't get over the idea of a God who regrets. I don't like the idea that God can have a change of heart, because deep down inside I wonder, "what happens if He changes His mind about me?"

I think the problem really comes down to the baggage that each of us have with the word regret. Somehow we have convinced ourselves that the word should be used to describe mistakes we've made or things that we'd do differently if given a second chance. However, the true meaning of the word is nothing like that.

Have you ever heard someone use an expression like "I regret to inform you that..." How can a person wish they had done something differently while simultaneously doing it in the first place? Once your brain recovers from that last sentence, you'll realize that one who uses regret in this way is simply acknowledging the heavy heart with which he must deliver some piece of news.

The true definition of regret in our language is to 'feel sad, repentant, or disappointed over'. This lines up with scripture as well as the word for regret here is the word "**nacham**" which means to "console yourself" or "to grieve".

Here's the truth: God doesn't change (Malachi 3:6). The bible says He's the same yesterday, today and forever (Hebrews 13:8). James 1:17 says that with Him there isn't even a "*shadow of turning*". His love never ends and the same love he displayed for you on the cross 2,000 years ago he offers you today.

Hopefully you will be able to see as I do that the heart of God that is on display here is not one of judgment without mercy. Rather, this is a deeply hurtful and personal experience for God. Necessary, yes. But still hurtful. Nearly every person alive at the time, people He created in His image and loved unconditionally, would be wiped off the face of the earth. It had to be so, in order that He could save them from themselves, but the act of it broke His heart.

My comfort through all of this, is that I serve a God who grieves about the evil found in this world even more than I do. It makes me realize that we are not alone, and more importantly, that we are not home yet. I hope that he finds me faithful as he did with Noah. However should I ever stumble I am reminded that while God grieves for me and "regrets" any sin I commit, I know he wants to take that grief on himself for me. He doesn't want me to live a life focused on the *"sin that so easily besets us"* (Hebrews 12:1) because he came to give me an abundant life that can only be found in surrender to Him.

Genesis 7

You would think that when you're trying to stuff just enough animals on one boat to ensure their future procreation that God would appreciate a pragmatist. After all, this is no time to get our feathers ruffled just because we forgot some traditions for a few months.

What we find instead is that God did not just include enough animals to allow for future offspring. He actually commanded that a larger number of "clean" animals be taken...

"Take with you seven pairs of all clean animals..."

Genesis 7:2

This begs the question, "Why the special treatment?" Are clean animals really worth more or just "better" than their unclean counterparts? Perhaps they are more fragile and God was just hedging his bet?

No, in fact there was a divine purpose in the bringing of "clean animals."

You see Noah and his family would need much more than just food and shelter to survive. They also needed their God. The way that man connected with God back then was through sacrifice. It was vital to a life lived in relationship to him.

It is, therefore, fitting that God would make a way to keep Noah's family not only safe and well-fed but also connected to Him. Like the other animals, some of the clean ones were meant to carry on their species through procreation. Still, with 7 pairs of each, it would seem as though God had provided enough for Noah's family to continue to offer sacrifice, which we find he did, in Genesis 8:20.

"Then Noah built an altar to the LORD and took some of every clean animal and some of every clean bird and offered burnt offerings on the altar."

Genesis 8:20

No matter what circumstances you find yourself in, make a habit of giving (your time, talents and treasure) to God. Sacrifice is as vital to our development as it was to Noah, and needs to be a part of our lives as often as possible.

Genesis 8

Have you ever listened to someone's story of faith and wondered "why doesn't God work like that in my life?" More specifically, have you ever heard one of these faith giants recall a time when God "spoke" to them and wondered "why don't I hear from God like that? If God speaks to people like that and I'm not hearing him, is my faith not deep enough or am I really a Christian?

If that's you, I want to encourage you to take a page from Noah. After all, he was found to be the only righteous man on earth at one time. Surely he has the market cornered on what God is saying to him right? If he needed to know something, he'd just ask and God would open the heavens and in a booming voice deliver the message right?

True there was a time when God seemed to speak directly to Noah...

> *"Then the Lord said to Noah, "Go into the ark, you and all your household, for I have seen that you are righteous before me in this generation."*
>
> **Genesis 7:1**

However, we aren't told how this message was delivered. Was it a voice booming and loud or still and small? At the risk of challenging the specific words, I would ask was it a voice at all? What if God gave Noah this message not through audible words but simply the spirit confirming something to Noah in some intangible way?

The reason I ask is that we spend so much time focusing on Noah's faithfulness before the flood that we might miss how he discerns things after.

The first question he has is, "when am I supposed to get off this boat? I was told when to get on, but when is it time to leave?" Apparently the one window in the ark could not see the land and this was going to be a big discernment issue. Open the door too early and he could sink the boat.

So what does he do? He sends out a bird and it comes back with nothing. He sends out a bird again. Again it comes back with nothing. All the while praying. All the while saying "God I'll do what seems to make sense to me and when you give me a peace about moving in a certain direction, I'll know that it's you and move."

He sends out a bird again, and it comes back with a olive branch. Notice this...that would seem to signify to me that the litmus test for dry land has passed with flying colors. But he waits. Noah has experience in the discernment department and knew, before the prophet Isaiah wrote about it, that "those who wait upon the Lord shall renew their strength."

A fourth time he sends out a bird. It does not return. Noah meditates on this and finds that peace welling up in his heart. He recognizes that peace...it's the same Spirit that brought him this far.

Perhaps that is all a bit of speculation into the nuances of what happened but the larger facts remain. God speaks to us in different ways. For many of us, including myself, it has never been an audible voice but that has not lessened its impact. I have learned to recognize the voice of my shepherd through experience with Him.

I encourage you, if you are facing any decision, pray without ceasing, do what you have a peace about, don't do what you are hesitant about, and wait for God to speak.

Genesis 9

When we are purchased by God, our lives ransomed with the life of His Son, we are eternally set free from the penalty that we deserve as a result of our sin. Furthermore, God is forgiving and the things which we have ruined here on earth can also be restored. For example, if we hurt people in relationships as a result of our sin, God can heal those hurts and restore the relationship.

Having said that, I have noticed that many times things are never truly the same. God desires to make all things new, but if feels at times that when he does, some vestige of sin remains - a reminder that this world is still broken until God truly restores everything to Him.

Such is the story of Noah in Genesis 9, which starts out with God renewing a blessing that He made when He first created man. That man would be fruitful and multiply and replenish the earth. Everything that he made for the first generations of man would now be passed on to Noah's family and be given for their enjoyment. In fact, perhaps for the first time it would appear that meat would be on the menu for dinner.

Yes everything seemed to be back in its place. Noah even took up gardening and planted a vineyard. Then, all of a sudden a moment of true humanity changes everything. Noah, enjoying the fruits of his labors has too much to drink. It was a moment of weakness and he was full of nothing but a desire for his own satisfaction. That's really the root of all sin isn't it? It's about us and how to fulfill our own desires regardless of the consequences. The Bible is pretty clear that drinking to the point of drunkenness is sin but Noah indulges himself and does it anyway.

As a result, we have a scene that some of us may not fully understand. There are simply too many unanswered questions. Did Ham stumble mistakenly into his father's tent and find him that way? Did he look on his father with disrespect or even lust? Did he do anything to him as some legends would suggest? We simply don't know what the exact sinful action was here, so we can't deem it to be important otherwise God would have told us. What we do know is what led to it and must assume that **is** important. Noah made a mistake, and as a result, a chain reaction was started which led to his family being torn apart. It would appear that this relationship was never restored, and the pleasure of a moment brought a lifetime of consequence.

I would summarize by saying this, that if we have been bought with a price, our eternity is secure in spite of any sin we may commit moving forward. I cannot stress this enough, You are forgiven. You are forgiven. **You are forgiven**. However, our motivation to abstain from sin should not come merely from a motivation to worship God and thank Him for what He has done. We must recognize that all sin, while being set free from eternal judgment is still subject to earthly consequence, and while this life is truly a vapor, it will only appear that way on the other side of eternity. Let's not make the mistakes that cause so much pain to us and the people we love.

Genesis 10

This is the second chapter in the Bible's first 10 that functions simply as a family tree or ancestral document. It's awfully difficult to get that for your daily reading and expect to walk away feeling filled. I admit, I struggled with it myself, and began searching everywhere for answers. I looked at specific words in the original languages, read commentaries, and then as a last resort, did what I always do when I don't know what do with a passage. I tried **asking questions**.

It's really important that we develop a habit of asking questions. It's really the best way to learn. Let me give you an example. I know how to play guitar. In fact, I've taught several people now. I could walk up to person A and tell them "I'm going to teach you to play guitar" and as long as they're willing, I'm sure we'll achieve some measure of success. However, if person B walks up to me and says "I noticed that you play guitar, can you teach me?", I have a pretty strong gut feeling about who is going to be more successful in the end, as the passion of the learner has more impact than that of the teacher.

My high school math and science teacher began every year with the same speech. It was about something he called "GANAS" which apparently means **desire**. He would write the word with big letters on the board and then proceeded to explain that too much is made of the teacher's ability to present and the learner's ability to pick things up easily. In fact, too much is made of ability in general. "However", he would say, "If you have GANAS, I can teach you."

The same is true of God's Word. How much we get out of it depends on our desire, and our desire for it is shown by the questions we ask of it.

So I came up with a question. If Noah's sons proceeded from the Ark to populate the world, then which one of his sons did the line of Jesus come from? After all, I figured much is made of Jesus' lineage and these records seem to be important enough to Jewish history that I assumed that information was available. We can begin our search with the book of Matthew where the bloodline of Jesus is recorded all the way back to Abraham in chapter 1. So, we simply need to know which line Abraham came from and that's pretty easy by simply reading Genesis 11:10-26.

Jesus, and all Hebrew people come from the line of Shem. That name became the root word for "semitic" as in "semitic languages".

So what can we take from all of this? Perhaps there is something we're missing, and perhaps years down the road I will stumble upon something that causes me to look deeper and a light bulb will go off for me. But for now, I will lean on my favorite quote from Oswald Chambers,

Plainly put, the exercise of opening a chapter like this and anticipating or expecting God's Word to reveal truth to us and not return void is perhaps the very point of any study of the Bible. Often it's not about how much we learn, it's about how much more we come to expect of it each time we open it. The more we get, the more we want. God's Word is perhaps the only thing on earth that we can't consume in excess. There is no chance of getting too much of it. It is food for the spiritually starving and that desire only increases once it gets a taste. Let's stay hungry, and passionately desire the Word of God.

"Oh, taste and see that the LORD is good! Blessed is the man who takes refuge in him!"

Psalm 34:8

Genesis 11

Here's a truth that I have learned over years of following Jesus - He actually does have plans for us and while he sometimes appears to leave the details up to us, He will take action to get us back on the right track if we veer off of it.

In chapter 11 we find this happening twice, and the chapter is bookended by these stories. Working backwards, consider the story of Abram at the end of the chapter...

> *"Terah took Abram his son and Lot the son of Haran, his grandson, and Sarai his daughter-in-law, his son Abram's wife, and they went forth together from Ur of the Chaldeans to go into the land of Canaan, but when they came to Harran, they settled there."*

> **Genesis 11:31**

I'm no Bible scholar, but Harran was not where they were trying to get to. So why did they settle there? Did they give up? Did they find in Harran something better than what they thought they might find Canaan? Was someone hurt and sick and they had to rest them for an extended period? Did they run out of supplies or money?

A bunch of things could have happened to prevent their journey to Canaan and the best we can do is speculate about it. Speculation should not be overused when asking questions about what the Bible says, but I do believe it has its place. I would guess that whatever the circumstances were, the true reason that Abram's family settled in Harran was that God did not want him in Canaan...yet. He would eventually deliver it to Abraham's descendants, but wanted to teach them first. God's work in our lives often happens on the journey to get to where we are going, not in the place itself.

Perhaps you have been waiting to arrive when you simply need to enjoy the process. God is working on you right now, and offers you the ability to be closer to Him during this time than you ever dreamed possible.

Unfortunately however, I have also experienced God's methods from earlier in the chapter. I would contend that while it may be hard when God steps in and says "not yet", the difficulty can be even greater when he allows us to have our way for a bit. There was a time when people had progressed so much that they just kept drifting further and further away from God. God permitted their progression to a point, but eventually had to step in. They were so far off the path he had planned for them that if they took one step further they would destroy themselves.

I've been there. I've grabbed hold of the reins and said, "God why don't you let me steer for awhile?" It wasn't arrogance as much as impatience. I needed direction from God, and when I couldn't hear it, I decided to take action. I justified it by telling myself, "I'll just get moving and see if God is up ahead of me. I mean, that's what taking a step of faith means, right?" In reality, what I really needed to do was wait. This mistake came at great cost to my family and me, but ultimately God intervened and lead me out of it.

Here's the deal though, now that I'm this side of it - I don't necessarily regret it. First of all, regret should be reserved for things we never try, not things we try and fail at. In fact, while I wish I didn't have to fall on my face to learn, I learned things through that experience that I could not have learned any other way. I can still sit back and know that while I may have run top speed into a brick wall and even burned the whole thing to ground, God made beauty from the ashes.

The comfort I offer you today is not that life walked hand in hand with God is easier. Actually, God will sometimes drag us kicking and screaming through the valleys. The comfort comes in knowing that while we might let go of His hand from time to time, He never lets go of ours.

Genesis 12

It is so important that we see God in every step of our lives. Sometimes we start out on a path so convicted of the direction God has called us to that we miss the journey. Sometimes the path that God calls us to has many detours and if we focus too much on the destination then we just get confused when we end up somewhere else or even worse, feel like there must be something we've done wrong because God has clearly abandoned us.

If that's you today, I want to encourage you to take something in from the life of Abram today.

"Now the Lord said to Abram, 'Go from your country and your kindred and your father's house to the land that I will show you. And I will make of you a great nation, and I will bless you and make your name great, so that you will be a blessing. I will bless those who bless you, and him who dishonors you I will curse, and in you all the families of the earth shall be blessed.'"

Genesis 12:1-3

God makes a promise to Abram and he sets out sure of where God is leading him...

"Abram took Sarai his wife, and Lot his brother's son, and all their possessions that they had gathered, and the people that they had acquired in Haran, and they set out to go to the land of Canaan."

Genesis 12:5

That seems to be the destination that God is leading them to. However, Abram doesn't end up there. He arrives there, but does not stay. Once there, God lets him know in a manner of words that he has other plans for him. What does Abram do? He leaves, and we must assume this too was under God's direction. But before he does, he builds an altar. He recognizes that this change in the game-plan doesn't mean something went wrong. He recognizes that the significance of a journey with God is not where you're going but rather who you're traveling with.

Abram moves to the hill country. And builds another altar. Again he recognizes that while his path has changed, his God hasn't. He moves again. And again. Why does he move? Perhaps God lead him some of the time. Sometimes he moved for practical reasons like famine. While he made some mistakes in his conduct in places like Egypt, we shouldn't assume that Egypt was a mistake. After all if your argument is "things didn't go well in Egypt so obviously Abram was out of God's will" then the same logic could be used when he left Bethel - "why would God lead him to a place that had a famine?"

The problem in Egypt wasn't that Abram went the wrong direction, it's that on that part of the journey, at some point he let go of God's hand. He started to fear man instead of God, and that's the true lesson we should take from it.

My encouragement to you is to just enjoy walking with God today. Picture it like a walk in a beautiful park instead of a walk on a highway. A walk on a highway gives you only two choices and you would have to assume that one of them is wrong. However, when walking in a park, stopping to smell the roses all of a sudden becomes appropriate, even normal behavior. Grab hold of Jesus' hand and try not to assume where you're going. Just enjoy the journey with Him.

Genesis 13

Abram's journey has seen many miles, many locations, and many altars. He he has gotten off track, circumstances in the family have caused him to wait when he wanted to go, he has been told "not yet" and been taken on detours, and now he is faced with what is probably his toughest decision. The land will not sustain both he and his nephew, Lot. They will have to split up.

Great is Abram's faith that God is in control at this moment. He is the elder in the family, so it could be said that it would be his right to choose first. He knows that God has promised him Canaan which lies just to the west. However, he yields that honor to Lot. Lot chooses east, and Abram finally makes his home in the promised land of Canaan.

There are applications for us in this story. First, the more literal among us will realize that this mildly echoes a New Testament story where ministry partners Paul and Barnabas end up parting ways. The dispute was not doctrinal, but was handled maturely with an agreement to divide and conquer.

Of course, a more generic application is simply this: sometimes we have to make very tough decisions if we want to follow God. Sometimes we have to choose between our head and our faith. These are never easy choices, but are always the choices that we look back on as the mileposts or better yet, the altars along our journey. They forever serve as a reminder of where we've been, where we're going and who has brought us.

When I read the story of Abram finally settling into the land that God has promised him, and when I reflect on the broken path that God lead him on to get there, I can't help but sing a few lines from "Canaan Bound" by Andrew Peterson. If you don't know it, I'd really recommend that you give it a listen...

Sarah, take me by my arm
Tomorrow we are Canaan bound
Where westward sails the golden sun
And Hebron's hills are amber crowned

Like the stars across the heavens flung
Like water in the desert sprung
Like the grains of sand, our many sons
Oh, Sarah, fair and barren one
Come to Canaan, come

Long after we are dead and gone
A thousand years our tale be sung
How faith compelled and bore us on
How barren Sarah bore a son
So come to Canaan, come

I can picture Abram himself singing this. Singing about a voice of "Love and Thunder" that compelled him through all circumstances to keep walking by faith. Abram's faith was rewarded with treasure and promise, and yet it is only a glimpse of what we as believers, the descendants of Abraham are promised as a reward for our faith. I want to walk by that same faith and trust that the God of Abraham and Jacob will also hold my hand and bring me to the promised land.

Genesis 14

There is so much that could be said about this chapter, mostly centered around the person of Melchizedek. He is a mysterious figure that is spoken of in both the Old and New Testament and deserves our attention, but let me be clear that much about him is unknown and susceptible to speculation.

The point I want to impress upon you is this, that God's Word contains everything that God wants us to know. If some details are missing, we should assume that they are not needed to understand God's message. Based on that theory, I want to focus in on a few details of this story, as well as Melchizedek himself.

This chapter recounts the first known war in the Bible. A confederation of 4 kings wages war on 5 kings who were a part of a rebellion. Lot was among them. The confederation won and kidnapped Lot and took all his possessions. Abram, being loyal to his nephew, then rallied his own men, all 318 of them and pushed the enemy back from their lands and reclaimed their possessions.

This is a remarkable story that certainly rivals the legendary underdog status of the Spartans. Abram, upon returning must have been tempted to revel in his own glory and leadership ability. However, his character has been tested before and here he shows an amazing display of humility and reverence before God.

He is met on the way back by the king of Sodom and the king of Salem, Melchizedek. This is an important encounter, as Melchizedek is later shown to be foreshadowing Christ himself in Hebrews 7. You really need to read that chapter to get all that God has for you on this, but allow me to highlight some of the more important points.

There is no record of Melchizedek's father, mother, birth or death. This makes him mythologically an eternal figure, which is an appropriate foreshadowing of Christ who is described in John as being from the beginning.

Jewish priests are all from the tribe of Levi, however Levi was not born yet so Melchizedek predates him, making him greater. Likewise, Jesus is also from the wrong tribe, the tribe of Judah. He is greater than any priest before him.

Melchizedek's name means King of Righteousness and he was the king of Salem which means King of Peace. Both of these descriptions are used of Jesus.

Melchizedek, then, is both priest and King—a unique combination that is certainly echoed in Christ.

We could expound on any of these points, and talk more of priesthoods and lineages and I would encourage you to investigate further into these things as they are fascinating. However, in keeping with the theme of offering a daily thought to ponder, I would invite you to focus on the gifts that are exchanged.

"And Melchizedek king of Salem brought out bread and wine. (He was priest of God Most High.) And he blessed him and said,

'Blessed be Abram by God Most High, Possessor of heaven and earth; and blessed be God Most High, who has delivered your enemies into your hand!'

And Abram gave him a tenth of everything."

Genesis 14:18-20

Abram has achieved much but wants to give honor to God for it. He wants to worship and so he gives a portion of his reward to Melchizedek, who has been ordained as God's representative in that he was a priest. That is Abram's gift to God. What is the priest's gift to Abram? He **communes** with Abram over bread and wine. This is so significant, as our high priest, Christ Jesus, on the night he was betrayed had **communion** with his disciples in much the same way. He spoke of the bread and wine signifying His body and His blood and that it must be broken and poured out for communion with Him to be possible. That is His gift to us.

One of the most exciting things that a believer gets to do is to honor God through giving. We can never out-give Him. No matter how much money we make, his sacrifice will always be greater than ours. However, like Abram we have the opportunity to show a gesture of our gratitude when we give to God. In this way, we honor Him and show our obedience and submission, the way Abram did before Melchizedek. Let's be the kind of people that recognize God as the source in our greatest victories and accomplishments by offering our gifts back to Him and to His work. This could be giving to your local church, or simply pouring out in generosity your time, talents and treasure to the people he loves—your neighbors, co-workers and everyone on the planet who was created in His image. It may never feel like enough, but honoring him in this way is a pleasing act of worship to Him.

Genesis 15

As I read through Genesis 15, I am reminded that the heroes of our faith really lived out their faith when put to the test. This particular story reminds me of Solomon.

I have always felt that the story of Solomon was unique. Solomon was found to be so righteous that the Lord wanted to reward him. God offers to grant him one "wish" and though He could have asked for anything in the world, he asks for wisdom. Wow. Here's a guy who has his priorities straight.

Notice something in his request though—Solomon isn't just asking for wisdom without purpose. A true man of God feels called to a mission and asks to be equipped for it. This is the heart of Solomon in his request. He doesn't assume the throne, but rather understands he received it because of who his father was. He is young. Very young. Too young, in his mind, to lead God's people, so his request is one of desperation. He has everything he could ever want, except something that money can't buy—Wisdom. His request still brings emotion out of me and stirs my own passion...

"You have shown great and steadfast love to your servant David my father, because he walked before you in faithfulness, in righteousness, and in uprightness of heart toward you. And you

have kept for him this great and steadfast love and have given him a son to sit on his throne this day. And now, O Lord my God, you have made your servant king in place of David my father, although I am but a little child. I do not know how to go out or come in. And your servant is in the midst of your people whom you have chosen, a great people, too many to be numbered or counted for multitude. Give your servant therefore an understanding mind to govern your people, that I may discern between good and evil, for who is able to govern this your great people?"

1 Kings 3:6-9

I am in awe of this kind of dedication to duty and calling, and I recognize that this is shared by other heroes including Abram. Abram has just returned from battle. He has wealth and land and the promise of God on his side. God promises a reward for his faithfulness, but Abram can think of only one thing he wants - a child. Now, those who have had difficulty bearing children will recognize this desire right away, but again, Abram is not just thinking of himself. He doesn't just want a child, he's really concerned about the future. He is concerned that the people who depend on his inheritance will fall under the rule of someone that he is evidently not a fan of.

Abram wants a son so that the influence of his faithfulness won't be limited to his mortality. He wants the opportunity to raise a child to fear God, as he does. God answers and says that not only will he have a child, but he will live a long life, and have the time he needs to instruct his son in the ways of righteousness.

Make no mistake, the way of righteousness is the way of faith, not works. Abram is not young, but without hesitation, he believes, and God "counted it (his faith) to him as righteousness".

Living lives worthy of the calling is important, and it is important to resist the devil and his temptations. Would you, however, really like to please God? Start believing that He can do great things. Believe He is powerful and that He will deliver.

> *"Without faith it is impossible to please God."*
>
> Hebrews 11:6

As we become more conformed to the character of Christ, I pray that our faith gets better and not just our behavior. I don't want to just live the Christian life. I want to experience life **with** Christ.

Genesis 16

If there is some low-hanging fruit, or most easily recognized moral to the story of Abram having a child with Haggar, it is obviously that the end does not justify the means. God will not bless our focused effort if our methods lack integrity. It's easy to see this in light of a clear-cut abandoning of the covenant of marriage that he has with Sarai. However, what if the situation wasn't so clear and was more nuanced?

I won't strain to come up with a different scenario for Abraham, but I will acknowledge this: there are times when the big picture is easier to trust God for than the details.

I can point to a few times in my life where I really felt like God was leading me in a direction, and even felt sure of what that direction was. Then came the hard part. Letting God do it. I know where he wants me to get to so I try to figure out how to get there. And this is where the nuance comes into play - it's easy in those situations to convince yourself that the actions you take must have been what God wanted you to do. After all, wouldn't our trust in Him grow if we took a step of faith and he met us there?

In reading again the story of Abram and Haggar, I see the situation differently and can at least empathize with Abraham's argument within himself. "Sarah has been barren. She is old. Her maid is not. God promised me a son. In fact, it would seem that

God's plans will be fulfilled through my seed. And hey, God said I would have a son, but he never mentioned Sarai right? If God left that detail out, then perhaps His will is for us to have this child through her maid. Plus it seems like Sarai wants me to do it..."

He sees the solution now as the obvious plan, because it makes sense to him. How else could God's plan be fulfilled under the circumstances? Yes, when in doubt the easiest solution is most likely the best.

This is the kind of thinking that leads to weak faith. When we remain pragmatists in our walk with God, we remove the need for miracles. In other words, we remove the need for God to work. When we can look back on a "journey of faith" and easily recognize how things worked, we rob ourselves of seeing God.

God only shows up in our rearview mirror when there is no other explanation. If we are determined to find a way ourselves, then we'll only see our own tracks when we look behind us. Let's let him do the impossible and wait for his prompting before taking a step.

Genesis 17

What do we do when we are broken from our failures? When the weight of our sin has driven us to depression. When things are crumbling around us and we know it is our fault? I, unfortunately, know too well the pain of Abram. I have sinned in ways that have hurt my family. I have failed in ways that have cost my church. What do we do when we realize that we have been the problem?

Our human tendency will direct us to curl up and hide from the world. We'll even convince ourselves that this message from the enemy sounds like the Godly thing to do. I say that from the perspective of a leader. When I fail, my first thought is "my church deserves better", or if at home "my wife can probably lead in this area better than I can so I need to give the reins to her". Truth is, my wife probably is better than me at a lot of those things. And the enemy will remind me of that every time I fail. Why? Because I've been called to those positions. I never earned them. God specifically chose me in spite of my weaknesses so that his power would be even more evident in what He does through me.

It is during these times that I want to quit. I want to step down. I want to, but I know I can't. Especially in my position. I will recognize that there are some cases where a pastor might fail, specifically in the area of public sin, and it leads to an appropriate resignation as his presence does more harm to the church. But as a general rule, if failure means you're no longer able to serve, then who will lead our churches? If I fail and tell my men I'm no longer fit to lead, what will they assume if they find themselves broken by inadequacy one day?

This is the position that we find Abram. Abram has failed. Miserably. His shame is too great to bear. If he is going to make it, God has to restore him, and do it quickly.

"When Abram was ninety-nine years old the Lord appeared to Abram and said to him, 'I am God Almighty; walk before me, and be blameless, that I may make my covenant between me and you, and may multiply you greatly.'"

Genesis 17:1-2

Got it. Don't make any mistakes. Good grief. So what is Abram's response? He falls on his face. He can't even lift his head from the weight of that command. Then God does what he does best...he restores Abram. If you'll allow me to paraphrase, God says to Abram, "I have given **you** a new name. **You** are not longer to identify yourself as a failure. As for the future, **I** will make you the father of nations, **I** will make you fruitful, **I** will subject kings to you, **I** will establish a covenant between us."

He then asks Abraham to make a one-time decision to commemorate this moment. He and all his household are circumcised. That seems like a huge ask, but don't think of it in terms of the obviously uncomfortable experience. Think of it in terms of it's fleeting nature. It's not something that lasts, because it doesn't have to. God doesn't need Abraham to do something every day for him. God promises to fulfill his covenant and challenges Abraham to do two things. Call yourself by your new name and ceremonially cut yourself off from the rest of the world. You are set apart and you need to identify as that, even if you don't act like it.

What do we need to do when we are broken? Stop identifying ourselves as merely failures. We are, in fact, more than conquerors because in spite of our failures, the God of the universe fought and won the fight already. We also need to be set apart. What that means for us today is not the absence of sin, but that we stand in opposition to it. That we identify what it is and who is behind it...it is an attack by the enemy himself. An attack on us and an attack on one whom God loves.

When you are tempted, don't focus on the fact that your flesh is weak. Focus on the fact that your enemy is attacking and wants to defeat you. That thought alone may give you the resolve you need. However, if and when you fail and are momentarily defeated, immediately rise and say "Where, O death is your victory? Where is your sting? I am more than a conqueror through Christ who loves me!"

Genesis 18

This chapter perhaps presents more questions than answers and therefore can be tough to gain any perspective from. First, we open with the fact that the Lord came to visit Abraham. He looked up, and saw three men standing nearby.

This is interesting because we are not told who these men are. First of all, are these men in addition to God, or do they represent Him? On one hand, one of the men tells Abraham that he will soon have a son, but then Sarah laughed and the text tells us that...

> *"The LORD said to Abraham, 'Why did Sarah laugh and say, "Shall I indeed bear a child, now that I am old?" Is anything too hard for the LORD? At the appointed time I will return to you, about this time next year, and Sarah shall have a son.'"*

> **Genesis 18:13-14**

The text almost reads as if the same one who delivered the news also responded to Sarah's laughter.

On the other hand, the men then set out from their meeting place and Abraham followed. The Lord again spoke, so perhaps

God was indeed represented by these three men. Or, at least one of them. It seems upon a complete reading that while there were three men, perhaps only one spoke and was referred to as the Lord.

Then of course we have this strange chain of events which begs to ask even more questions: first, the Lord looks upon the city of Sodom and indicates that he will go pay a visit to them...

"Then the LORD said, 'Because the outcry against Sodom and Gomorrah is great and their sin is very grave, I will go down to see whether they have done altogether.'"

Genesis 18:20-21

Then, the men head for the town but the Lord stays behind with Abraham...

"So the men turned from there and went toward Sodom, but Abraham still stood before the LORD."

Genesis 18:22-23

So what is going on? Are there four beings presents (the Lord and three men)? Are there only 3, with one who speaks? If so, did two men start toward the city with only the one staying behind? This seems to be the case in the beginning of chapter 19.

By the way, this was a bit of an exercise to simply demonstrate that it is important that we engage with the scriptures in this manner. We must develop the habit of always asking questions. When we ask questions, we demonstrate an appropriate respect for God's Word. We in effect treat is as "living" and assume that our unanswered questions do have answers. In that respect, we assume the infallibility of the scriptures. In essence, asking questions of God's Word demonstrates our theology as much as anything.

It is easy to imagine why God would reveal himself to Abraham as three figures (though two of them may have been angels), as we understand that God reveals himself to man as three persons. It is also easy to imagine why only one would speak, as each person in the Godhead has distinct responsibilities. Little is known at this point in human history about God with respect to any literature written about Him. They do not as far as we know possess any scriptures. However, Abraham's perspective is perhaps more in-tune than ours with who God is because God had direct contact with him from time to time. This passage says that God "communed" with him, which sounds like an absolutely amazing experience.

With all this in mind, I am willing to commit to these men representing God, and with that, I will relate the experience that Abraham had with God to the experience that God would desire with all of his people.

First, Abraham met with God and we can get a lot from the experience. Abraham recognized the presence of God and invited him to fellowship with him. We should do the same. Abraham prepared for fellowship by getting food ready and even asking those around him for help in respecting this holy time. It was a time of refreshment, beneath the shade of a large tree, with plenty of food to eat.

Second, God had a discussion with Abraham. Specifically, the fate of Sodom and Gomorrah was on the agenda. I do not believe that Abraham changed God's mind in this exchange. I do, however, believe that God showed compassion for the things that were important to Abraham. He recognized the mercy and love in Abraham's heart and it moved him. God is pleased when we worship in love more than burnt offerings.

I remain convinced that God's Word is always profitable (2 Timothy 3:16-17) and that there are rich truths on every page. We just need to keep asking questions. Sometimes the text will provide answers. Sometimes it won't...yet. The point of it all is that we get to a place where we always expect it to.

Genesis 19

Genesis 19 recounts one of the more sensational stories in the Bible. It's about one righteous man's life and a defining moment for him in the midst of a city full of wickedly evil people. True to the promise that he made with Abraham, God searches but does not find 10 righteous people in the city. However, he does protect Lot and his family from the coming destruction and allows them time to flee. This is, more than likely, what was most important to Abraham when he asked God to spare the city earlier: the life of his nephew, Lot.

I see in this passage the cost of following God. First, we notice that when God speaks and asks us to move, the time to do it is immediately. When we become parents, we quickly realize through our children that delayed obedience really is disobedience. We do see evidence of this in Lot, who even upon seeing the wickedness of the men outside and hearing a direct command from God, remains conflicted...

"When he hesitated, the men grasped his hand and the hands of his wife and of his two daughters and led them safely out of the city, for the Lord was merciful to them."

Genesis 19:16

Second, if needed God will drag us kicking and screaming to where we need to be. I have not found this to be universally true, but it may indeed be. The angels in the story grabbed Job's hand and forced him to flee. I do not think it is above God to use events in our lives, especially painful ones, to drag us away from what we have built up to be more important than Him. When we put things ahead of God - money, comfort, even our children - we worship them above Him. If God has set us aside for a special purpose and this is the state he finds us in, He is not above removing those things that have our heart's devotion. If we aren't willing to forsake all, He may indeed take all until we learn to trust Him.

"What hinders me from hearing is that I am taking up with other things. It is not that I will not hear God, but I am not devoted in the right place."

Oswald Chambers

Third, we can't look back. When you make the difficult decision to forsake all for the cause of Christ—not so much in terms of salvation, but rather a clear call to mission—the enemy will tempt you with thoughts of how much easier your life was before. He will describe a former life of plenty while you struggle in hardship. Lot's wife longed for the comforts of home and lingered behind him, resulting in her own destruction. These are moments when our resolve must be strong. I am reminded of the story of Hernán Cortés, a spanish conquistador who set out to conquer the New World with about 500 men. Upon arriving, the hardship of life in a foreign land was so great that his men began complaining and begging to go back home. So, Cortés did what he thought was necessary: he ordered the men to burn the ships. Return would not be an option.

Sometimes following God means putting everything in perspective. Daniel outwardly defied the king's decree. The disciples dropped their nets and left their families. The apostles risked their lives spreading the Word through missions work. It would appear at first glance that perhaps their decisions were made somewhat recklessly. Like they had failed to "count the cost". However I would suggest that one who truly understands the ramifications of following God or not realizes that...

> *"Greater is He that is in you than he that is in the world."*
>
> 1 John 4:4

Our resolve today should be to follow God wherever he leads. It may not be the safest place to be, but we should never feel safe with the alternative of wandering from what we know He wants us to do. God will do what he must to bring us back to His path—just ask Jonah.

Genesis 20

The great theologian John Gill, in an exposition of this passage wrote...

"Good men not only fall into sin, but have their relapses."

John Gill

It is more than interesting to see how God uses our mistakes and misfortunes to achieve his divine purposes. What his purposes might have been in the story of this chapter I doubt we can ever say for sure, as they could have far reaching consequences beyond what is even recorded in the Bible.

The question that I'd like to pose an answer to is this: When we are instructed to do something by God and we go our own way, what effect does that have on the purposes of God? The answer is, none.

Let me affirm that God gives us our own minds and we have the ability to make right and wrong decisions based on our moral consciences. However, God's ways are higher than our ways (Isaiah 53:9), and not just in turns of importance, but in terms of supremacy. The little bubble of freedom that we have operates only inside of the larger sphere that is God's will.

God has a plan and a purpose for everyone and everything. When we sin, we stand in opposition to his plan and when we do his will, we join him in accomplishing it. The book of Proverbs uses nice alliteration to put it this way...

"Many are the plans in a person's heart, but it is the LORD's purpose that prevails."

Proverbs 19:21

So now we finally take a look at the story of Abraham attempting to get along in society by telling everyone that Sarah is his sister...again. I believe that while God's disapproval is not so specifically implied in the text, we can still assume its existence. He obviously does not approve in a very general sense, as he inflicts punishment on the man who takes Sarah for his own, both here and with Pharoah in Genesis 12.

In a specific sense though, I do not believe that God told Abraham to perpetuate this lie, which we find out here he has been telling everywhere he has been. I believe that God could have protected him against any unruly man, the way he protected Lot and his family the night they left their home. I believe that if Abraham would have trusted in God, God's purposes could still have been accomplished and no harm would have necessarily come to him. However, the fact that Abraham fails under pressure does not mean that God will. Rather, he uses the failure of Abraham to bring about his plan, thereby redeeming

Abraham's actions. In fact, he uses the situation to bring about his purposes in King Abimelech's life as well.

When we decide not to follow God, it is not God's will that suffers but rather our own happiness. When we sin, we stand in opposition to God and his laws and fall out of sync with our Creator. However, we find our life is abundant and fulfilling when we align our heart and our way of life to God's ultimate purpose in redeeming mankind.

Genesis 21

If there is a theme in Abraham's life that keeps coming up but is often overlooked, it is submission. Submitting to others is something that he seemed to have no problem with, and it seems to have brought him favor his whole life.

He was in submission to God. Only a couple of chapters before this one, God made a covenant with Abraham and that covenant on Abraham's side was signified by circumcision. As an adult, he and all his men were circumcised. He circumcised his son Isaac upon his birth as well. Abraham's faithfulness was rewarded by the fulfillment of God's side of the covenant - to bless him and his offspring for generations.

He was in submission to his wife, Sarah. Here in the beginning of chapter 21, we find that Sarah is distraught by Ishmael, the son of Hagar, who mocked Isaac at a party in his honor. She asks Abraham to remove both of them from the protection of their home. Perhaps there was even more to it. Perhaps Sarah couldn't stand the sight of Hagar for having a child with her husband and had been fuming for years, with this event being the straw that broke the camel's back. Abraham was troubled, as I'm sure he didn't want to subject Hagar and Ishmael to hardship, but out of respect for his wife and to protect his family, he reluctantly sends them away. Abraham is blessed for this submission though, as

God promises to look after Hagar and Ishmael, thus relieving Abraham of his guilt.

Finally, we see another type of submission result in prosperity for Abraham when he meets with King Abimelech. Abraham was always in submission to the authorities of the land. Admittedly sometimes to a fault, but overall, we must assume that his general submission to their rule was God-honoring. We can say this, because of the words of apostle Paul...

"Let everyone be subject to the governing authorities, for there is no authority except that which God has established. The authorities that exist have been established by God."

Romans 13:1

This is a difficult verse to hear in America. We tend to be proud of the battles that we've fought and won for our freedom and with good reason. It would be inappropriate to say which of our wars were just and which ones weren't. The wars that we are perhaps most proud of, however, are the ones that have resulted in the rights that we all share today, among them, the right to overthrow our own government.

Perhaps there are times when this kind of thing honors God. Perhaps an evil ruler should be removed, and outright oppression should not be tolerated. However, a general, arbitrary disposition of defiance to government and the authorities that lead them is not right. The leaders of this world have been ordained by God for some purpose or another. Jesus never taught about overthrowing the state, but did say something about rendering to Caesar what is due to him. One might even suggest that the most practical modern-day interpretation of this means that you ought to pay every dime that you owe in taxes.

Even in the most ungodly segments of our culture—yes, even in our American government—God is still working. In the part of our lives that lack most in spirituality—like politics—God can still teach us something.

Submission to authorities teaches us to trust that God is ultimately in control.

So let's get right down to it: what does this mean for us today? How should we respond in our culture, in our time? You might ask, "what exactly do you want us to do, not speak up in politics? Not join political parties? Not run for office?"

Of course not. In fact, what you see in Abraham's life is that God used his submission to bring about change in the government's position on things. Abraham had shown over years to be a man who respected Abimelech, so the King meets with Abraham as he is gaining influence to work out some sort of mutual understanding. Abraham uses this platform of influence and brings the King up short on what would appear to be a civil matter about the local water supply. He is able to persuade Abimelech to reverse course on this particular action and the King moves his entire army out of the land as a result.

So how do we know when it's time to take action? I will leave some of those questions up to you and let you prayerfully consider them. I'd personally start with this: as Christians, we should not speak badly about our president or other elected officials. We should pray for them. I'd even take a one-for-one deal at this point. For every time that you think badly of, or discuss in a negative way about, or post on Facebook your displeasure toward our elected officials, you have to say a prayer for them. AND you have to do it in the same audience. If it's just you thinking badly about them, say a private prayer. If you've talked with someone badly about them, grab that same person or another church member and invite them to pray with you. Or, you may find yourself in the latter camp, in which case your heartfelt prayer needs to be blasted across your social media channels without any ambiguity or sarcasm. I don't believe that God would consider a prayer that is laced with passive reproval toward someone else as one that is sincerely a request about His will being done.

If we all committed to that kind of challenge, one of two things would happen. There would either be an overwhelming outpouring of prayer for our government officials or we'd all find much better things to talk about. Either way, God's name would be more glorified in our lives and I think that's kind of the point of all of this, isn't it?

Genesis 22

Along with submission, it is obvious that there is one central theme that runs throughout Abraham's life—Faith. He is not always found faithful, but God is constantly challenging him and his faith can be seen growing with each victory that exists among the failures. Here though, God presents him with his greatest challenge.

First, note that Abraham might have had feet of clay when it came to faith opportunities earlier in life, but after being delivered and blessed by God many times, his faith has grown and is ready to be proven by fire. He tried to solve his problem of being heirless on his own when he and wife agreed that he would bear a son with Hagar, but after God rebuked him and then delivered Isaac to him through Sarah in their old age, it would appear that Abraham is on a totally different level of faith.

You would think that after waiting so long nothing could be more important to him than his son. However, something was more important - his faith. He believed that Isaac was truly a gift from God. He believed that God had some greater purpose for him than simply being an heir to provision. He would be an heir to a promise.

It would seem that Abraham's decision to sacrifice Isaac was on such a level of faith that it is seemingly too far out of reach for us to grasp any hope of our faith ever being that deep. However we can't miss the point of Abraham's faith as displayed here: he knew very little about what was about to happen. In fact, he may have even questioned whether or not he would be able to go through with it. Who knows how long he held that knife, tears streaming down his face, trembling at the weight of the challenge that was set before him.

Abraham didn't know how he was going to perform, and that is the point. He knew only that he could trust in God, if not in himself.

> And Isaac said to his father Abraham, "My father!" And he said, "Here I am, my son." He said, "Behold, the fire and the wood, but where is the lamb for a burnt offering?" Abraham said, "God will provide for himself the lamb for a burnt offering, my son." So they went both of them together.
>
> Genesis 22:7-8

God will provide. What if we don't have the strength? God will provide. What if we get lost and don't know what to do? God will provide. What if we can't provide? God will provide.

I can't imagine the number of questions that must have raced through Abraham's mind as he marched his only son up that mountain. What I can imagine, is that only God knew what it would be like. In fact, this moment in the Bible was to set the stage for the day when God would march his own son up

Calvary's hill, not as one to be saved, but as one who would be the sacrificial lamb for all mankind.

Interestingly Abraham places the wood on Isaac's back. The element of wood symbolizes humanity or man. Isaac bore this symbolic material up the hill to the place of sacrifice. Isaiah 53 paints a similar picture of the Messiah...

> *"Surely he took up our pain, and bore our suffering...he bore the sin of many, and made intercession for the transgressors."*
>
> **Isaiah 53:4,12**

Christ bore our sin upon his back. Isaac is the picture of Christ marching up the hill. Then he becomes the picture of man—you and me—upon the altar, when a substitute is found, or better yet provided so that neither Isaac, nor anyone else who believes in his name should ever perish, but rather have everlasting life. Thank you father, for providing for my freedom with the blood of your son.

Genesis 23

Our lives our filled with journeys. Some are short and some are long, but all of them eventually come to an end. The memories I have about the journeys I've traveled are not so much about the places that I went, but rather the people that went with me.

I have considered myself fortunate to have had so many great companions for my life's biggest adventures. I have loved the people that I have served with in ministry and cherish the memories that I have made with them. I am acquainted with the heartache that comes from inevitable partings after meaningful seasons with each other. The reality is, people move on, people get sick, and of course, people don't live forever.

What I've found most difficult to adjust to is life after my companions are gone. I grow to be dependent on the people that God has placed in my life. This brings me to my sorrow for Abraham and anyone who has ever lost a spouse: I can't imagine a life without my life's partner, my wife.

Sarah has died, and she leaves behind her husband and her only son. Abraham is left to mourn and to try to figure out what he is to do next. Perhaps fitting, is the place where this happens.

If you recall, when Abraham and Lot parted ways, Abraham settled in Hebron...

"So Abram moved his tent and came and settled by the oaks of Mamre, which are at Hebron, and there he built an altar to the Lord."

Genesis 13:18

This was to be the place that he would live. The place that God would promise him as far as his eye could see in every direction. As he sat there that day, in the shadow of Hebron's hills, in the shade of his wife's tent, in the presence of her body, he must have remembered what it was like the day he received that promise from God. He remembered what it was like to tell his wife, to celebrate with her, and to plan for their future together in the land.

All journeys must come to an end, but most difficult for him was the fact that Sarah's journey was now over and his journey was to continue. Every journey of significance to this point had been made with her by his side and each one was made more special because he had shared it with her.

So how does God convince us to move on when we are dealing with grief or tragedy? I believe one way is by taking us back to where we started. It was God who made Sarah, then known as Sarai. It was God who ordained the circumstances of their meeting, of her becoming his wife and of them settling in Canaan. It was God who changed Sarah's name, who promised them a son and delivered on that promise, and who ultimately provided a substitute sacrifice that would save his life.

On his last night at home before undergoing heart surgery, my grandfather was trying to convince my grandmother not to make the long trip to the town where the hospital was located. She told him that she didn't want him to go along, to which he replied, "I'm not going alone." She asked, "what do you mean?" My grandfather, who until that point was not a believer to our family's knowledge, responded by saying "The same one who brought me this far will take me the rest of the way."

My grandfather had been accompanied by my grandmother for most of his life. Whether or not he knew he wouldn't come home or even see her again, I am not sure, but I know this: at some point in his life, perhaps only in his final days, he became aware of who his true companion was in life, and this brought him great comfort at the end.

If you've lost or been parted from someone, take comfort that the one who brought you together will continue to walk with you and promises to reunite those who believe in him one day.

Genesis 24

I have meditated on the story of Isaac and Rebekah for a while and find myself unable to pick a theme to write about. I'm simply torn between two ideas. A part of me wants to remain in the themes that I've written about elsewhere in this book—of surrender to God's ultimate control of and plan for everything—and the other part is thinking just as a father.

On the one hand, you have here another amazing story of faith in God's providence and absolute abandon to the idea that he will provide a way. Abraham's servant heads back to Abraham's home country to find a wife for his son...but how do you do that? How do you convince a father, let alone a mother to let one of their daughters go with some stranger to be married in a foreign land to someone they don't know? Of course Abraham's servant isn't worried about that. Do you know why? Because those are just details. He has his priorities in order and knows that the most important decision is choosing the right girl.

I can certainly learn something from that as I typically know what the priority is at first, but it is quickly lost as my head starts swimming with questions of "but how is it going to happen?" So I try to make it happen. For example, I could be faced with a call from God to go somewhere and be a missionary. Perhaps God might even appear to me in a burning bush and say "I want you to take my gospel to another country." However, what happens once the flame goes out and the bush is no longer talking to me while I'm left with my thoughts? What am I thinking? How am I going to live? How are my kids going to get education? How do I keep my family safe? I ask dozens of questions about my future but fail to ask the most important one: where does God want me to go?

If you can relate to that, and want to know how to get out of that kind of habitual response to the call of God, then perhaps I can help by delivering some truth: You will never be able to focus on where God is calling you until you learn to trust Him with the details. We should simply be asking "Where, Lord" and trusting that wherever that is, he will also be and will provide for us. We should head into every directional call from God knowing only that where there seems to be no way, he will make one.

Yes this message of faith is certainly in the text of Genesis 24, but another part of me is just a father of a little girl, and when I think of Rebekah, I can't help but think of my son and daughter.

I love how Abraham has high standards for his son. So much of our focus tends to be on finding the right kind of man for our daughters, but how often do we speak of finding the right kind of woman for our sons?

As a parent, you want your little girl to grow up like Rebekah. Beautiful, respectful, kind, compassionate and pure. You hope that your parenting will lead her spiritually this way. All along, though, you know that you're not doing this so that she can thrive on her own later on. Rather, you have this sense that you are preparing her for someone else.

My heart goes out to Rebekah's father. I imagine the news hit him like a ton of bricks if not that night, then certainly the next morning when Abraham's servant thinks it's time to go already. What I must assume is that Rebekah's father feared the Lord, and out of reverence to him raised Rebekah up for such a time as this, knowing full well he would one day have to let her go for his service.

I pray that God can make me into that kind of father, for my daughter's sake. I want to be able to say with sincerity that while she is my little girl, my pride, my joy, she is not mine at all. I want to be able to give her to the Lord and because of that I pray that he is already writing another story in a godly young man's heart so that one day their stories can be combined and they can start a new chapter together.

In the end, these two thoughts on the passage are obviously woven together in my personal life. When considering my daughter's future choice in a partner, I understand that the priority is that she choose a Godly man. So what do I do? I typically go right to the details of "But who? Who is raising Godly men that I know? If no one, we need to change that! Someone start a young men's Bible study and mentoring program or something!"

You see, I've once again focused on the details that are far into the future where I can't possibly control them. What is the priority? That my daughter CHOOSES a Godly man. How about I simply teach HER that's what SHE needs to do, and while I'm at it, show her what a Godly man looks like in my own life. If I do that and leave the rest up to God, perhaps I'll find out that he really does know best and has it all in control.

Genesis 25

A theme that has been creeping up as we continue through the book of Genesis is that of God's providence. In today's doctrinal circles, this can be somewhat of a point of contention. If God is sovereign, then how much free choice can we really have? Wouldn't any of us having any free will limit the total sovereignty of God on some level? However inconsequential our lives may be, absolute sovereignty means just that: every single thing in total submission. Rather than continuing to avoid the issue, we are afforded the opportunity to look at it here in a different light—that of the rights of inheritance.

When one reads the Bible, especially the Old Testament, and sees what we would consider peculiar behavior for a human being, we must understand that the people in the Bible are living at a different time and in a different culture. It can be difficult for us to relate to these people, when reading about how they treat their children and how some are blessed and others seem to be looked over. Are they really playing favorites? Is love for our children not a universal value that spans culture and history? I would say it is and would also say that this is not contradicted in the Bible.

We have to imagine a culture where your inheritance was typically given to the firstborn. When that child was born, they became the target of your influence, education and affection.

This was not because you necessarily like them more than your other children, however. This was because as firstborn and heir to your inheritance, you want to make sure that you teach them how to run it wisely.

In a sense, Abraham's focus on Isaac at the expense of his other children is really in the region's best interest. Do you remember how Abraham treated the people that worked for him earlier? He understood that his wealth was the source from which everyone around him was sustained. He had a responsibility to them as well. Abraham comes off of the pages of Genesis as an incredibly generous benefactor, full of a sense of responsibility that surely came with the wealth that he possessed.

As Abraham grew older and looked around at the people who depended on him, he knew he needed to provide a way to bless everyone. He did this by choosing to invest in Isaac. He circumcised him to symbolize a covenant between himself and God. He was willing to sacrifice him to show his faithfulness to God in all things. When his mother died, Abraham took great care to choose just the right woman for Isaac so that he would have a life companion, just as his father did. I'm sure he poured into Isaac and reminded him of where they had come from. He would have shared of his successes and his failures. He made Isaac his chosen one, not to play favorites, but for the good of all the people.

What gets lost in the discussion of God's right to sovereignty is his purpose. It is fact that only God is God. He alone made the universe and everything in it. He gets to make all the rules. He has the God-given right to do so. God can choose to favor one group of people over another. In fact, he does. He sets apart the Jewish nation and displays his mercy toward them and showers his blessing upon them. If you look at the course of human history, the Jewish nation was as sinful as any other nation that existed at any given time. Yet he deliberately chooses to bless them, deliver them from their enemies, increase their territory and refer to them as his chosen people.

At this point, some would ask, "why?" and in response, some hardline, reform-doctrine christians might suggest "it doesn't matter..." or even that it is inappropriate to question God as his purposes are higher than ours. I love my reform friends but it is important to ask why, especially when considering God's sovereign choice, because it is the heart of the Bible.

Much like Abraham chose Isaac for a greater purpose than just playing favorites, God had a special purpose in choosing the nation of Israel. While at first it may seem that he simply favors one nation over the rest of the world, out of this nation he would deliver a Messiah who would come to save the whole world.

A study of God's sovereign will is important to understanding the lengths to which God will go to redeem the one he loves. It speaks of his foreknowledge, wisdom and compassion in a way that would leave any understanding of them incomplete without it. Today, bask in the glow that God's plan for your salvation has been an eternity in the making. By choosing Israel, he was choosing you.

Genesis 26

The apple doesn't fall far from the tree. That's a bit of a joke we tell whenever someone's kids do something that reminds us of their parents. Typically this is more along the lines of some harmless, possibly idiosyncratic behavior if mentioned out loud, but it is a phrase also used under one's breath when a particular vice seems to have been passed down from the parents.

However, if we consider the fullness of this horticultural (yes, I just used that word) metaphor, we can find ourselves tremendously challenged by it. Every piece of fruit is an extension of its parent. It may blossom into its own one day, but all of its life-giving genetic code was provided by its parent. This idea goes beyond genes though, doesn't it? If we are to draw any human conclusions from this analogy, we need to recognize that the circumstances surrounding the apple's upbringing greatly affect it as well. What kind of weather was common at the time? Did it get enough water? Did its parent struggle through hard times (like drought)? Was it barren for one or more seasons as a result? In the end, was the apple tree able to provide the kind of nourishment that an apple needs to flourish on its own?

That rather long-winded introduction was simply to setup the following: Isaac was a product of his father's upbringing. He apparently learned a lot from dear old dad. He learned how to cultivate the ground. He learned how to dig for water in an otherwise desert land. He learned commerce. He learned how to coexist with others in the same land. He learned how to put down roots and make a place a home. He learned how to love a woman. He learned how to fear God.

Of course, we don't just pass on good things to our children. One only needs to listen to *"Cats in the Cradle"* by Harry Chapin to be reminded of the negative impact we can have on our kids when our priorities are in the wrong place. In Abraham's life, he made a few mistakes of his own and Isaac didn't exactly learn from them. Rather, he fell into the same kinds of traps.

In today's modern world, a person who grew up in an abusive home is far more likely to abuse their spouse. Alcoholism is almost assuredly generational, and we tend to go the same churches and vote for the same political parties as our parents do. For guys especially (though much of the same is true for women), we will find that our children will speak to our wives the way that we do. They will speak to their children the way that we speak to them.

Our conduct in the home has lasting, generational results.

Isaac found himself in the same land, under the same king, with the same circumstances as his father. As he settled in Gehar where King Abimelech still reigned, he felt he could be in jeopardy because of the beauty of his wife. Never mind that it was God who told him to stay put; Isaac, like so many of us, after hearing from God and following his direction then grabs the reigns at the first sign of trouble. He, like his father before him, had an achilles heel when it came to trusting God with his safety in a foreign land.

"When the men of the place asked him about his wife, he said, 'She is my sister,' for he feared to say, 'My wife,' thinking, 'lest the men of the place should kill me because of Rebekah,' because she was attractive in appearance."

Genesis 26:7

Where do you think he learned this trick anyway? Of course from his father. What we are not told is whether or not Abraham introduced the concept to him as a viable tactic. Abraham should have learned from his mistake after making it the last time, but in the midst of chaos, we all tend to run back toward what we feel is most comfortable and not what is right.

No, we can't say what Abraham taught his son about this issue, and certainly Isaac made up his own mind in absence of his father. What we can rejoice in however is that in spite of it all, Isaac's life was not defined by this incident. This would not be a referendum on Abraham's parenthood. On the contrary, Isaac shows much integrity after being asked to leave by the king. He digs a well that belonged to his father, but the people say he does not own the rights to it. Wanting to be above reproach, he digs again and gets the same response. He moves on again and this time, there are no objections. He showed incredible patience in waiting on the Lord through this ordeal and as a result, his riches flourished. The king eventually comes to make a pact with Isaac. The same pact he made with his father, Abraham.

Apparently the apple doesn't fall far from the tree, so let's determine that if this saying is ever used of us, it will be for our children's victories and not their defeats. Let's take that as a challenge and not cower away and stop trying just because we've made some mistakes. Our kids lives are bigger than a couple of bad decisions. Let's grow, tall and mighty in spite of our circumstances. Don't use them as an excuse. Let's be branches that are attached to the true vine so that we can provide the kind of nourishment that our kids need to develop strong character, moral values and a love for God.

Genesis 27

It gets easier to sin the more you do it.

Let me clarify in case you wonder what I mean by 'easier'. I mean that there is less conviction or guilt with each occurrence and therefore we find it it 'easier' to continue in our behavior.

Perhaps the most tangible example I can give is that of lying. Actually, we tend to not think of the sort of lying that I'm talking about as 'lying' per se. Perhaps we would prefer the term 'fibbing'. A moment where perhaps we don't tell the whole truth. I call them snowball lies myself. Snowball lies start out with something small. I say 'small' because they usually feel either inconsequential or even more appropriate than telling the full truth.

For example, perhaps your wife has had a rough day when she comes home. The last thing you want to do is is show her the unexpected bill that came in the mail that day. After all, the bill will be there tomorrow and will have different meaning for her after a good night's sleep. Seems harmless right? Okay, so what happens if she asks if you and the family can go out for dinner that night instead of cooking, and you know your budget is tight enough that the bill changes the answer to that question? What do you do then?

I would suggest that the minute your wife comes home and you think to tell her about the bill and don't for the reason already given, you have sold out. You've sold out to putting one value over another. You've convinced yourself that because you love your wife and want to make her happy, there are times when it is appropriate to hide things from her. Make no mistake, if you know about it and she doesn't, you're hiding it from her. You have decided that sometimes happiness is more important than honesty in a marriage.

Okay so I know that last bit sounds harsh. Of course you're not trying to intentionally deceive your wife. On the contrary, you feel you are caring for her the best way that you know how and I guess that's the point that I'm trying to make: Snowball lies will never appear like real lies and will even resonate as being the most 'moral' option at times. This is why they have the potential to become like a snowball rolling down the hill, picking up size and speed over time.

Rebekah had this problem. She believed Jacob to be the chosen one. Let's go ahead and give her that one for a moment. Let's say for the sake of argument that Jacob was the one whom God wanted to receive Isaac's blessing. She knew this and also knew that Isaac couldn't help but love Esau more. Isaac was, in her mind, blinded from seeing what God wanted because of his partiality toward Esau. So what does she do? She 'helps' him make the right decision.

In her mind, this is justified. Not only is Isaac not able to see his error, but as his wife, it is actually her responsibility to correct him. So there she is – convinced that action must be taken. It's important enough that it needs to be done by any means necessary, so she convinces Jacob to trick Isaac into giving him the blessing instead. Jacob has some objections at first, but Rebekah is convicted and ready to take responsibility if it goes wrong...

> *"But Jacob said to Rebekah his mother, "Behold, my brother Esau is a hairy man, and I am a smooth man. Perhaps my father will feel me, and I shall seem to be mocking him and bring a curse upon myself and not a blessing." His mother said to him, "Let your curse be on me, my son; only obey my voice..."*

Genesis 27:11-13

Of course, this is pure nonsense. How can she take responsibility? Everyone involved is old enough to know that we're all responsible for our own actions. When Esau finds out, it causes such a family uproar that it is Jacob, not Rebekah, who has to flee at once and live somewhere else. Meanwhile, the snowball is still growing, and Rebekah has to explain why Isaac has left. She blames it on the selection of women among whom they live. She points out the wisdom of Isaac living somewhere else. She probably isn't even thinking of this as a cover-up at this point. She is actually probably convinced now that it truly is the best thing for Jacob. "Perhaps" she thinks to herself, "Perhaps this whole thing went wrong because God wanted Jacob to leave and this was the way he chose to orchestrate its happening."

You see, in the end snowball lies don't just get us off track, they can convince us that the track we're on is still the right one. The Bible tells us that God causes everything to work together for the good of those who love him (Romans 8:28). However, we should understand that to mean that God works in spite of our mistakes, not that God wants us to make them so he can work through them. In other words, God can be glorified in spite of our sin, but we never glorify him in our sin.

In our lives, we will have many opportunities to make clear choices about right and wrong. However, we will daily have many more choices that seem to be slightly more nuanced because of their circumstances. It's not just lying, it's the everyday things that we all struggle with. Paul explains a few of these things to the churches...

"For I fear that perhaps when I come I may find you not as I wish, and that you may find me not as you wish—that perhaps there may be quarreling, jealousy, anger, hostility, slander, gossip, conceit, and disorder."

2 Corinthians 12:20

"Let there be no filthiness nor foolish talk nor crude joking, which are out of place, but instead let there be thanksgiving."

Ephesians 5:4

Let's not sacrifice our moral integrity on the altar of pragmatism and 'being real'. Let's not condition ourselves to be immune to conviction by a pattern of behavior that weakens its effect. Let's be children of light who walk convinced of a higher calling.

Genesis 28

There is a very interesting bit of business mentioned here about how God wants his people to live with their eyes fixed upon his promise. Isaac, after following his wife's advice, decides to bless Jacob and send him on his way. Again, I do not believe it was God honoring for Jacob to deceive his father, but as we've said all along God uses our failures to bring about his purposes in our lives. Here is Isaac's blessing to Jacob...

"May God Almighty bless you and make you fruitful and increase your numbers until you become a community of peoples. May he give you and your descendants the blessing given to Abraham, so that you may take possession of the land where you now reside as a foreigner, the land God gave to Abraham."

Genesis 28:3-4

Did you catch that? His hope for Jacob's future is that he would come to take possession of the land as a foreigner. You see, Abraham didn't grow up in the land. He moved there and took possession, as a gift from God. God, through providence and provision, gave the land to him. Isaac again settled in the land as a foreigner. However, Jacob grew up there. In that sense, he would be the heir to it. He would receive it through his birthright.

The problem is that the promised land would become the symbol for the ultimate riches that God will deliver to all his sons and daughters. The promised land, was indeed received through "promise" and not property rights. Jacob would become one of the 3 patriarchs most often mentioned when referring to the God who would make good on his promise. The "God of Abraham, Isaac and Jacob" had promised and delivered the land to both Abraham and Isaac, but if Jacob was to be the standard-bearer for the God who fulfills his promises, he too needed to have his own experience of this.

God uses this time in Jacob's life in a mighty way, and we can learn a lot about how we ought to live from it. True, we can learn that God delivers on his promises and in fact wants us to live a life where we actually experience what it means to live by faith. For Jacob, God has him abandon the land that would be rightfully his so that he will recognize God's provision when he reclaims it. This experience would grow Jacob's faith immeasurably.

However, there's a second component to Jacob's exile that is more fully understand in its New Testament application—that of living in the land as a foreigner. Hebrews summarizes the entire generational story in a few short sentences...

"By faith Abraham, when called to go to a place he would later receive as his inheritance, obeyed and went, even though he did not know where he was going. By faith he made his home in the promised land like a stranger in a foreign country; he lived in

tents, as did Isaac and Jacob, who were heirs with him of the same promise. For he was looking forward to the city with foundations, whose architect and builder is God."

Hebrews 11:8-10

God promised the land to Abraham and his seed. However, they recognized that for a time, many generations in fact, they would prosper but not truly possess the land. They were in a period of waiting and relying on God, constantly looking forward and having faith that he would deliver them. During that time they lived in tents or tabernacles which is really to say that they lived in temporary shelters, awaiting a time when their permanent residency would be fulfilled.

This is how we are to live today. We are to be constantly recognizing that our current place in this world is temporary. In fact our bodies, like tents, are temporary. Paul actually refers to our bodies as "tents" and expresses the same sentiment of temporary living...

"For we know that if the earthly tent we live in is destroyed, we have a building from God, an eternal house in heaven, not built by human hands."

2 Corinthians 5:1

We look forward to a day when God will deliver us and clothe us in perfection. We will inherit the true spiritual home that was promised to the descendants of Abraham. Until that day, we are strangers living in a foreign land, and we must live as though we don't belong to it. Our challenge is to not conform to the pattern of this world, but live lives worthy of the calling. Peter expressed it this way...

"Dear friends, I urge you, as foreigners and exiles, to abstain from sinful desires, which wage war against your soul. Live such good lives among the pagans that, though they accuse you of doing wrong, they may see your good deeds and glorify God on the day he visits us."

1 Peter 2:11-12

Living "called out" lives, different from the world around us, glorifies God. It signals to both the world and to each other (in the church) that another kingdom exists, the kingdom of heaven. The kingdom of heaven is at hand, and the proof of that is found in the foreigners, the sojourners who live in this world, but are not of this world.

Genesis 29

God has a way of using the meek and mild to accomplish his purposes. This is a theme that exists throughout the scriptures and many of the most important moments in God's unfolding story of man are accomplished by those who are meek in spirit.

John the Baptist was a sort of messenger who came on the scene to "prepare the way" for Christ. He preached to crowds that they should "Repent! The kingdom of heaven is at hand!" He started to gather a following and probably had every reason to be somewhat puffed up. After all, he was the leader of this somewhat organic movement. Before "Occupy Wall Street" there was "Occupy the Holy Land" and John was its leader for a time. Whatever following that continued to pick up steam behind Jesus certainly got its start with John. So great was his influence that Herod had him killed. Yet, John wore this banner lightly, and when Jesus' fame was brought to him he simply stated that "he must become greater and greater and I must become less and less. In fact, his message to the people was this...

> *"After me comes he who is mightier than I, the strap of whose sandals I am not worthy to stoop down and untie."*

> **Mark 1:7**

There was no doubt in John's mind who the real star was, and when that light began to shine, he quietly faded to allow its full brilliance be on display. John was certainly the epitome of humility and God used him mightily.

During a time when the Jews were in great danger, Esther and her cousin Mordecai were given placement in the Persian king's palace. They had influence and certainly had the king's ear. When the king's right-hand man Haman showed a genuine dislike for Mordecai, he devised a plan to get rid of all the Jews and tricked the king into signing it into law. You would think they would have immediately gone to the king to put a stop to it. However, we assume that, through God's providence, they bit their tongues until just the right time. When they did approach the king, it was with respect and not demands. As a result, not only was Haman hanged and the Jews saved, but Mordecai was given the highest office in the land next to the king, and at the height of the Persian empire, which was in control of the land where the Jews lived, God had placed two of his most humble people right beside the king to ensure the survival of the Jewish nation.

Joseph also, was one who had a quiet manner about him. He was slow to speak and quick to listen. He was betrayed by his brothers, framed by a woman and spent time imprisoned. Yet he never turned his back on God and God raised him up to do a mighty work. Like Mordecai, he rose from that humility to a position as the king's right-hand man and led the Jewish nation before it was a nation.

Interestingly enough, Mordecai was from the tribe of Benjamin. Benjamin, of course, was Joseph's younger brother. He was known for his humility as well, being the youngest of 12 brothers. In fact, both Joseph and Benjamin learned humility from their mother. Their mother, was Rachel, the chosen wife of Jacob.

Rachel was not the eldest daughter. We see her first come on the scene as a shepherdess. Why was a woman tending to Laban's flock? Laban had sons, but perhaps they were not old enough yet. Leah was the eldest, but she couldn't do it on account of her vision problems. Rachel took it upon herself as her duty. In many ways she stepped up when Leah could not.

However, when Jacob fell in love with her and asked for her hand, her father tricked Jacob into first marrying Leah. No doubt Rachel would have known about the deception as it's hard to keep those kinds of marriage celebrations secret in such a small town. Yet, she does not object. She accepts her place as the younger sister, even though she's been taking on the responsibilities of the firstborn. Rachel's humility seems almost foolish doesn't it? We read that story and practically beg her to stand up for herself. However, her humility is used mightily by God as well.

I'm a huge "Lord of the Rings" fan. At it's heart, the story is about how even the most insignificant person can change the world.

Delving deeper, we find that sometimes the people who make the biggest difference have no idea at the time. They are simply living their lives guided by their moral values. In the case of Bilbo Baggins, when ultimately faced with the chance to kill Gollum, the creature who tried to kill him earlier, he looked on Gollum with pity, and that pity stayed his hand. That's important when considering the providential undertones in the book. If Gollum hadn't lived, then the final scene in the book would not have happened and the enemy would not have been defeated. This is what prompts Gandalf to say...

"The pity of Bilbo may rule the fate of many."

Gandalf the Grey

The bottom line is this: if things didn't happen the way that they did, then perhaps Joseph wouldn't have had 10 older brothers. There would then be no one to be jealous of his favor in Jacob's eye. There would be no selling of him as a slave and no coming to Egypt. These are necessary events, not just for the life of Joseph but for the entire nation. After all, it is Joseph who makes the wise plans to prepare for the years of famine that were to come. Had it not been for him, the nation would have starved to death, and this includes Jacob himself. It was largely Rachel's humility that set these things in motion, and once again God's providence is on display in all its glory. He takes the mistakes of some to bring about the events necessary for his chosen people to accomplish his purposes here on earth.

Solomon was given the opportunity to ask for anything he desired and he chose wisdom. It made sense as he was the leader of the nation. For me, at this time, I choose humility. I pray that I can have the kind of humility that God has used for thousands of years to do his greatest work, so that through me he might be glorified.

Genesis 30

I would suppose the easier thing to write about in this chapter would be that of Rachel and Leah making the same mistake that their grandmother, Sarai (later called Sarah) made. They both at times battled seasons where they were unable to conceive and bear children. I know firsthand from friends and family how troubling this can be for a woman. Even in today's age of smaller families and more work outside the home for women, a woman often finds herself incomplete if she is unable to have her own children.

The theme of course that runs generationally in these women's lives is that it can be awfully hard to trust God when we want something so badly. We feel we need to try to do everything we can, to have a plan, to not give up, but to keep working at it. The problem with that of course, is that if God has different plans for us then we are almost sure to miss out on them. For example, what if God wanted us to fill our home with other children that have no home of their own? What if he wanted us to sacrifice the idea of our own flesh and blood for someone else who has no family at all?

If the stories of the patriarchs have one central theme, it would have to be faith.

That brings me to Jacob, and this very odd, some would even say weird, almost hippy-style breeding of his flock and how he became a man of faith.

By now I'm sure you've picked up on the fact that Jacob is a bit of a heel. Of course he is. That's what his name suggests. He is a bit of a shyster—a con-artist even—and seems to have no moral conscience when it comes to stealing from others. Sure, his father and grandfather had their moments and certainly no one is perfect. However, Jacob seems to have a major character flaw here and doesn't seem like one who can be trusted.

I personally feel that way about Jacob and when reading about his life, I can't help but wish that we had a more reputable role-model in him. However, out of submission to God's Word, I have forced myself to reflect a bit more on the facts of his life, and I know that I can't overlook this one redeeming quality: he stayed in the home of his father-in-law for an awfully long time and I'm not sure that he didn't have any other choice. He wasn't there under threat, and he had certainly served past his "contractual" obligation by now. He seems to exhibit a similar quality to his grandfather, Abraham. Remember when Lot and Abraham separated? He gave Lot the first choice of where he would settle and Abraham took whatever was left over. He trusted in God's providence and provision. Jacob, by the same token does something similar here when Lot insists that he stay longer. He could have said no, so without looking over his faults, let's give credit where credit is due. Jacob respected his father-in-law.

Of course he feels that it's time to start increasing his own territory so that he can leave an inheritance for his children's children. What follows is a bit of a mystery that we are simply left to speculate about. He tells Laban he will stay if he can have all of the speckled and striped animals in Laban's flock. He even agrees to watch Laban's flock and vows to keep only the offspring of the speckly-striped troupe that are his. Laban agrees and gives Jacob the first few animals of his very own flock. Jacob then takes branches from poplar, almond and plane trees and peels strips of bark off of them in a striped pattern. He set these branches near the watering troughs whenever the stronger of his flock were in heat. As a result, they give birth to offspring that is strong and marked with spots and stripes. His flock is multiplied greatly because of this.

Some have suggested that Jacob was a master breeder and there was a scientific reason for what happened. I personally think that has the possibility of robbing us of the true lesson we can take from Jacob's life. I believe that Jacob's rather bizarre tactics were spirit-led. I believe that in spite of Jacob's circumstances, God leads Jacob and gives him special instruction. When Jacob listens, God rewards his obedience by blessing him financially.

I would never want to suggest that we shouldn't be decent moral people. We are instructed in God's Word to treat others better than ourselves, and Jacob is a total failure on this front many times. However, I can't help but ponder this reality: God seems to look more favorably on obedience than simple moral behavior.

Now, I know what you may be thinking: "isn't moral behavior obedience as well?" Yes of course. Moral behavior comes from obeying the instructions for living found in God's Word. We are told how to behave and a heart fully surrendered will exhibit certain fruit in his or her life. There is a different kind of obedience found here though...that of being obedient to something unseen.

Every great hero of faith was given the opportunity to trust God when it didn't seem like a sensible choice. Noah was challenged to build a gigantic boat to save creation from a world-wide flood. Abraham was challenged to offer his own son as a sacrifice to God. Later, Moses would stand up to an entire nation. Daniel would be challenged to disobey the king's command not to worship God. David fought the giant. The disciples left their jobs and their families. Paul turned his back on the Pharisees. In all of these stories, following God seemed destined for hardship, and yet these mighty faith warriors were all rewarded for stepping out when the path forward was unclear. Worse, it actually seemed very clear that they were stepping off of a cliff only to fall to their end.

Have you ever felt challenged to really step out in faith? Not just to live a life worthy of your calling, but rather to follow a particular calling? How did you respond? If I could be real for just a moment, let me confess that I've had this happen to me in the last couple of years and while I started out well, I flamed out and shrunk back to what was comfortable as soon as the going got tough. I must confess, I'd really like a do-over.

Luckily for me, I serve a God of second-chances. My prayer today is that if I am given a chance again to follow Jesus into a great faith adventure that I will fear being out of his will more than the unknown. I want an adventure—the kind that takes place on the road less traveled walking with my Savior.

Genesis 31

I feel like I have narrative whiplash when reading this chapter. In spite of the many reasons to question Jacob's character, the fact remains that he is God's chosen one and I certainly expect for the unfolding story to feature God directing him in his efforts to overcome any of his adversaries. Stories make a lot more sense when there's a clear "good guy" and a clear "bad guy". We can then get behind the hero, identify with both his virtues and vices and cheer him on in spite of his shortcomings. In the absence of truly good "behavior", it can be tough to know who we are supposed to cheer for in the last few chapters of Genesis and I suppose the easiest way to identify them is to simply pay attention to which one God is speaking directly to. Which one is being led by God.

Well, "Houston we have a problem", because there seem to be two guys in a pretty important fight and neither seems to be selling me on why I should pull for them. Sure, Jacob seems to have been shafted by Laban lately, but Jacob's done his share of shafting before. Both have family and property in the balance. And most confusing of all, God is speaking directly to both of them!

These are the kinds of stories that frustrate me...that is of course, until I meditate on it and see that this is my story. More appropriately, this is our story. Both men seem to have some valid points. Neither is perfect and their mistakes have caused each other to stop trusting the other. There is no coming to terms as neither will concede to the other. So how do they get past it? Forgiveness. After everything they've been through and done to each other, Jacob and Laban realize that too much is at stake. They make a covenant and deal with it. There is some recognition on both parts, as well as plenty of affirmation to go around. They both recognize that no one is perfect, but they both serve the same God who seems to be leading them toward some kind of reconciliation.

We resemble this story much more than we know. We like to pretend that we live in a world of black and white. Perhaps this is appropriate some of the time. Certainly truth is black and white. Jesus is the only way to heaven. Every single person in the world deserves freedom. These are virtuous things and should be stated as absolutes. However, we have to be able to mature in our relationships with other people to the point where we can recognize that when it comes to conflict with each other (especially in the church) there are very few (if any) absolutes. We are never completely innocent, but are quick to say we are completely right. Anyone who has actually listened to a couple of friends tell both sides of the issue can understand that most of the division is a lot more nuanced than the two parties (we) would like to let on.

The world is not black and white. Mostly, it is simply filled with people and people tend to not get along very well. They tend to make much of little when it comes to having something against someone else. This is especially true of the church and we tend to divide over the silliest things. This is troubling and awful, and quite simply breaks the heart of God.

Did you know that we find Jesus wept more than once in the Bible? He wept at a funeral for Lazarus (John 11:35). He wept for the city of Jerusalem when he saw it before his triumphal entry (Luke 19:41). There was another night in which the Savior's heart was very heavy. It was his last night with his disciples. He had a lot of things on his mind, I'm sure. There was so much he had yet to tell them, but there was so little time. During his last meal with them, he looked toward heaven and prayed. Everything that was troubling him and everything he was feeling was poured out to the Father. He made mention of a few things in that prayer, but among them was a cry for unity...

"My prayer is not for them alone. I pray also for those who will believe in me through their message, that all of them may be one, Father, just as you are in me and I am in you. May they also be in us so that the world may believe that you have sent me. I have given them the glory that you gave me, that they may be one as we are one—I in them and you in me—so that they may be brought to complete unity. Then the world will know that you sent me and have loved them even as you have loved me."

John 17:20-23

He could have spent the time teaching them how to organize the church, but no, he trusted us to figure that out. He could have explained in exact detail what would happen during the end times, but I'm sure he felt that would all work out in the end. No, he used his time wisely and prayed for the thing that we would need help with the most. He prayed for us to get along. He prayed for us to love each other. He prayed for this, because in his mind, the world's reception of the gospel hinged upon it.

*"By this everyone will know that you are my disciples, if you **love** one another."*

John 13:35

As I read the story of it now 2,000 years later, I am convicted. I am troubled because I wonder how much we are hindering the mission of the gospel by fighting amongst ourselves. I have to admit I thought that our country's morality was going down the tubes because of the evilness of our culture. I have to wonder now if we are the ones responsible. I thought our nation was doomed because of unbelief. Now, I see that their unbelief is due at least in part (perhaps a very large part) to the church's behavior. Not individual clean living, but rather communal behavior. We simply do not do this whole unity thing very well.

"The greatest single cause of atheism in the world today is Christians: who acknowledge Jesus with their lips, walk out the

door, and deny Him by their lifestyle. That is what an unbelieving world simply finds unbelievable."

Brennan Manning

It's an often-used quote that I feel is really applicable to this subject. I wonder if the reverse can be true? Can the greatest revival and response to the gospel be caused by a church full of imperfect people who love each other perfectly? If we dedicated ourselves to unity, would we see God's spirit poured out on the world in such a way that we'd give Pentecost a run for its money? What I wouldn't give to see that day in my time. It starts with me. It starts with you. God make us one.

Genesis 32

Among the adjectives we have used to describe Jacob, we can now add two more to the list.

First, he finally achieved ultimate humility. It is no small thing that the same man who hatched various schemes to achieve wealth only to lose it all and have to fight for it now attaches that success to God and not his own planning. As Jacob says,

> *"I am unworthy of all the kindness and faithfulness you have shown your servant. I had only my staff when I crossed this Jordan, but now I have become two camps."*
>
> **Genesis 32:10**

For what it's worth, Jacob finally matured and is now practically an example of what it means to follow God. However, his humility does not define him completely. God makes us all unique. We each have differing skills, strengths and personality. God designed us and we must assume that his purpose in doing so was to use our individuality for his glory.

So it is amidst this truth that we find another adjective to describe Jacob...scrappy. Jacob is a fighter. He doesn't even know how to spell the word "quit" let alone have any personal acquaintance with its nature. He served 7 years in the house of his father in law so he could marry Rachel, and when Laban cheated him on it, he served another 7. He will not quit if he feels passionately about something and he was certainly passionate about Rachel. When I say that Jacob won't quit, I'm not saying that he merely gets up after each hit. He actually gets up and has a plan in place that he immediately executes each time.

It's true that Jacob sometimes receives direct word from God about what he should do. It's also true that many (if not most) times we should wait on God to reveal a plan to us. However there are some times, as was the case with Peter, where God's call to faith requires us to simply get out of the boat and start walking on the water. Do you understand the metaphor of walking on water? Have you ever tried to actually do it? It's somewhat unstable isn't it? At best, we would be completely unsure of our footing if we were ever asked by Jesus to walk on water. In those moments the only thing that we know is where Jesus is. Our eyes have to be fixed on him, because if we were to look at the path that we were on, we'd freak out. The sight of him is the only way that any of it could possibly make sense.

Jacob only knows that God has made a covenant with him. He prays and asks God to honor that covenant. In a sense, Jacob is not asking, but rather confirming with God that because of that covenant he will continue walking forward even though the path in front of him (concerning Esau) seems sure to end in death. You see, he could have gone somewhere else and settled down. He could have avoided his brother forever. But Jacob knew that he must inhabit the land of his forefathers, because that's what God told him to do.

I like to think that the wrestling match at the end of the chapter is more about God reminding Jacob of his strength rather than testing his resolve. I don't think that God actually needed that fight to understand Jacob's capacity. Rather, perhaps during a night when Jacob was unsure of himself, God reminded Jacob that he still had a lot of fight left in him. It worked too, as Jacob, who only a day earlier was humbly asking God to simply honor a covenant he already made, was now asking boldly asking God to bless him. The humility was still there, as Jacob acknowledges that his life was spared and not that he won the fight (v. 30). But there is strength as well. Jacob has been restored and reminded of who he truly is. The guy who never gives up. It's part of Jacob's design that God will continue to use for his purposes.

We can take a lot from this story and it will reach each of us on different levels because we're all made different. We need not be afraid of our personality as God has a plan for that. God is also made strong in areas that we are weak. We shouldn't focus on what we lack, but rather focus on this truth...whatever God's purpose is for our lives, God designed us specifically for it.

Genesis 33

Have you ever had a relationship fall apart in a big way only to be restored again? I'm talking about the kind of "falling-out" that results in years of separation from and perhaps hostility toward each other? What was it like when you were able to mend the relationship? Was there a huge weight lifted off your shoulders or did it feel more like you were getting past something. Did you feel like something was finally behind you or did you look forward to future? Perhaps you wondered "why didn't I do that sooner?"

Whatever the case might be, few of us have experienced this kind of thing on the level that Jacob and Esau had. If you've had difficult relationships in the past, perhaps you've learned some of the same things I have—that the problem is magnified when it's family, for example, and that was certainly the case with these two brothers. All the typical sibling rivalries are certainly compounded by the jealousy that inevitably comes when the parents so obviously favor one child over the other.

Of course there's the fact that the dispute was also about money. How many families and friends have been driven apart by a dispute over finances? We tend to judge each other's character by how we spend our money and lending money to family or friends is always a recipe for disaster. Is it any wonder that such a sharp wedge was driven between Jacob and Esau when Jacob basically stole Esau's entire inheritance?

How about the fact that in spite of the shortcomings of his character, Jacob went on to prosper? We hate to see the people that wronged us end up so happy don't we? Wouldn't we rather see them live out their days in sorrow for what they have done to us?

If you can't relate on some level to the disagreement between Jacob and Esau then you should count yourself fortunate. I don't believe, however, that many of us could claim to have escaped this particular tragedy. In fact, it's all too prevalent in families and in churches. After all, a church is a family and familiarity breeds contempt whether last names are shared or not. We are surrounded by broken relationships and past regrets. They haunt our memories and rob our joy. We are reminded of them by Satan on a daily basis. They cause us stress and can literally make it difficult to breathe.

I can't imagine the relief, joy and peace that Jacob must have felt as his brother Esau came running toward him and wrapped his arms around his neck. For the believer, this moment can be extra sweet as it provides the hope that while God has been working on us through a torn relationship, he has also had his hand on the other person and has been leading them toward reconciliation as well.

In the book of Revelation, Jesus, the lamb, says "Behold I am making all things new" (Revelation 21:5). Actually what is really conveyed there is that he is making all things new **again**. In other words, he is fixing what is broken. It is an acknowledgment that he has the power to restore things to the way they should be because he's the one who made them in the first place.

Only God has this power. That is why after this amazing turn of events, Jacob builds an altar and calls it El Elohe Israel, which means "The Mighty God of Israel". Wouldn't you like to do the same? Wouldn't you like to celebrate God's power in putting right what was wrong? If so, start with this – forgive those who have wronged you, ask forgiveness from those you have wronged and let God do the rest.

God designed you to be unique. He also designed you to live in community with others who are unique in their own right. The goal is not for us to be, act or think the same. The goal is that we can simply bow down and worship the same God.

Genesis 34

Sin will always play on our basic human tendencies. We already have the desire somewhere deep in our hearts to go there. The enemy just needs to tempt us. This is why, by the way, that Jesus could be "tempted" and yet not sin. There was simply no hint of sin anywhere in his soul. There was no foothold for the enemy, nothing he could sink his teeth into.

When we consider the lives, mistakes, faithfulness and failures of the patriarchs, it can sometimes be very difficult to see who is in the right and who is in the wrong. In fact, as I'm sure you've realized by now, it's almost always that way. No one is untainted by the experience. No one has been born any different – at least not in the sense of a propensity to sin. Everyone has it in them. Everyone is capable of a certain level of poor judgment and disobedience.

When we read the horrible story of the rape of Dinah, we can all probably relate on some level to both Jacob and his sons. You may find that you relate to one more than the other and that's fine. That is most likely a product of your personality and experiences. But here's the question: who was right? Or, in the discussions that follow, who made the better argument?

Let's review the facts: Dinah is raped and then her attacker's father comes to Jacob with a request that she be released to his son as his wife. A generous offer is made to Jacob, after which his sons devise a plan – actually, it's more of a scheme – and using their deception they manage to kill every man in the city and take the women and children with them.

Afterward, a confrontation ensues between Jacob and his sons. Jacob is furious, as his son's actions have put him and his family at risk. The sons argue that they should not tolerate their women being treated like that. Both are right, and both are terribly wrong.

Jacob is older and knows something his sons don't. Our actions always affect other people. If we so quickly take revenge when someone wrongs us, the consequences could be even further pain suffered by the people we love. This is Jacob's point, not that his own life might be in jeopardy but "I and my household...". Having said that, Jacob is most likely just too quick-tempered to get along. He will always have that self-preservative tendency to look out for number one. In his past, he has done this at the expense of his character, and perhaps this would have been much of the same had his sons not intervened.

Levi and Simeon on the other hand, were indeed too reckless in their behavior. Theirs was an overreaction to say the least. It was simply not a proportional response. Their sister was defiled, so every mother, daughter, sister and wife in town would pay by losing their son, father, brother and husband. Every man they had ever known would be wiped out in a single day. Would that really right the wrong that had been done to Dinah? But...would it have been better to give her over to her attacker to be his wife? After all, when a man is bold enough after this act to say "just name your price", what he's really saying is "I'm not taking "no" for an answer".

I believe the problem is that the more we experience the ways of the world without a healthy dose of God's Word to counteract its effect, the more worldly we become. The loftier idea of morality (knowing right from wrong) soon becomes something else called moral conviction (what feels right or wrong), which is another term for personal morals (I decide what is wrong), which is another way of saying I make up my own rules (my way is right). In this alternate reality, we tend to justify everything that we do for one reason or another. What some might point out as a misstep in our lives can easily be explained if they truly knew our side of the story.

What we must remember is that sin will always play on our basic human tendencies. If it feels right, don't do anything. This isn't about feelings. There are moral absolutes, and though I have certainly failed and not lived up to the principles that I claim to have, I know this after coming out the other side: it is never wrong to do right. It is never right to do wrong. My best advice? Listen to your conscience. If you find yourself in one of those situations where your morals are questioned, bail out immediately on the side of doing what you know is right. Pick up the pieces of whatever happens next afterward. Honest mistakes can be corrected. You can grow and learn from them. However, when we err on the side of diplomacy – and in doing so compromise our morals even the slightest – we do something to our soul that is more permanent than we'd like to believe. Don't corrupt your soul, feed it. Make an appointment to feed on God's Word today and ask him to help you fight the good fight.

Genesis 35

If you fall off of a horse, the idea is to get right back on, right? Sounds almost easy, but I've actually fallen off of a horse at top-speed, and let me tell you the only reason I got back on was pride. There were people watching me, and I wanted to look tough. It's much harder to get back on the horse when God's the only one watching. We know he is forgiving and that he must understand how hard it is. However, we must also know that he wants to see us ride again.

Jacob has certainly had some tough times and just when you think you're seeing a glimpse of change in his life, he falls even harder than before. In fact, there is only one thing that is consistent in Jacob's life with God...God himself. God continues to overtly reveal himself to Jacob. No matter what Jacob's done, God's not done. He has a purpose for Jacob's life and it will be realized.

Jacob comes once again to this place called Bethel. Guess what? That's not its real name. The real name of the city is Luz, but Jacob calls it Bethel. Why? Well, for starters, this is where God has repeatedly revealed himself to Jacob. It started during a time of shame, when Jacob had to leave his family for fear of his brother's wrath...

"Early the next morning Jacob took the stone he had placed under his head and set it up as a pillar and poured oil on top of it. He called that place Bethel, though the city used to be called Luz. Then Jacob made a vow, saying, "If God will be with me and will watch over me on this journey I am taking and will give me food to eat and clothes to wear so that I return safely to my father's household, then the Lord will be my God and this stone that I have set up as a pillar will be God's house..."

Genesis 28:18-22

The word "Bethel" means "House of God". Notice that he starts his journey by laying a stone, which he calls a pillar. A pillar is but the start of a mighty building, and ever since then God has been building Jacob's faith one stone at a time. Every time he fell, God was there to help him up again and each time he was adding another stone to the mighty structure he was building in Jacob. God is a careful, particular builder. He doesn't rush, as he's more concerned with the finished product than he is with the time it takes to get there.

Think I'm being too metaphorical? Was he really just marking a place he'd come back to later? I don't think so. If he did, he'd come back and simply find that stone again. Instead, he lays another stone, or at least many stones to form an altar. This is simply what Jacob does when he meets God. He builds an altar every time to signify the name that he gives this particular place – the House of God. What is the house of God? I would suggest this. It's not a physical place. I say this because if Jacob had indeed found the place where God was, why would he ever leave? He did leave. He didn't stay in "Bethel"...or did he? It is my belief that Jacob had stumbled on a truth that the Psalmist David would soon put to music in the 23rd Psalm – *"Surely goodness and mercy will follow me, and I will dwell in house of God forever"*.

If something follows you then you are moving. If you're moving, you're not dwelling anywhere, at least not in the physical sense. The House of God not a specific place, but any place where Jacob encounters God. In fact, it's this truth that carries Jacob throughout his life and it can do the same for you. Imagine, being outside the safe walls of your church and yet having the confidence that God is ever-present wherever you are. You don't need a building or place of worship to meet with him. The place where you stand is holy ground!

The house of God is where God is, and it's where God does his best work in our lives. Jacob is laying stones every time he meets with God, both physically (as he builds each altar) and more importantly, spiritually. God is in effect building in Jacob his own temple or dwelling place, and he won't stop until he's done.

I remember a song that I used to sing when I was a child...I won't quote it directly as I don't want to diminish the weight of the message with children's rhymes, but the essence of the song is this: God took just a week to make the entire universe, and yet he's not even finished with me yet. He's still working on me. He's still chiseling off the rough edges, smoothing out the bumps. He's taking his time...why? Because I'm his masterpiece. A work of art that he wants to enjoy forever.

Oh, how he loves us.

Genesis 36

While this chapter concludes with another line of descendants, there is a bit of a story here of which we can ask some significant questions. Jacob and Esau are, by this point, both very wealthy. Having reconciled, they are now living in the same area. However, their wealth continues to increase to the point that it becomes very apparent that the land will not support both of them. Their cattle need grazing areas, and their farmers need fields to work. It's simply a problem of space – there really isn't room for both of them. So Esau moved his family away from Canaan to settle far away in the hill country of Seir.

This was a smart thing to do. A good businessman will rightly tell you that competition brings out the best in companies. However, this is only true when there is a sufficient market for both companies to exist. If there are only enough resources for one to thrive, then the only way to succeed is to either move from a competitive mode to an annihilation one, or join forces under one company. If the latter is not an option, then your company's success will depend on the other company's failure. When this happens, there is a clear winner and a clear loser.

Perhaps this is easier to explain using businesses simply because they aren't actual people. We can be somewhat nonchalant about our characterizations and absolute in our thinking when we are talking about things that shouldn't hold emotional sway with us. However, when family is involved, it takes on a whole new meaning. Imagine if you and a close family member were finally together after years of enmity between you. You are looking forward to the future together and then realize that you can't stay together because if you do, one of you will end up broke. There's not enough land or money for you both to prosper. What would you do?

Most likely, you would respond with something like "we'll figure it out…" or "there must be a way". Perhaps you'd try to consider some sort of mutual partnership. You'd try to do anything except the smart thing because this is about family, right? It's difficult to make a decision that would actually be best for the family when the peripheral consequence of that decision obviously separation.

I've thought about this a lot before concerning churches. I grew up in a very different area from where I currently serve, but both places have something unique in common. All of the churches are grouped in the same area. They are literally in competition with each other. The problem is not just that it causes many of them to struggle, but rather that it distracts them from Kingdom building. Each church is so focused on growth within the body that very few resources are set aside for taking the gospel out to people who don't have it.

A philosophy of divide and conquer would be more appropriate in the church today. If we were somewhat more strategic, I believe our method of growth would naturally be to introduce new people to Jesus, not introduce a new church to believers.

I know that was a bit of a rant, so let me move on to explain what I think is necessary for this to happen. It's so easy to point out a problem without offering a solution. To solve this problem, one of the key players needs to display great humility. Esau displayed a certain kind of virtue by moving his family away. Reminiscent of his ancestor, Abraham, who deferred to Lot when choosing where each would settle, Esau, whose original birthright was stolen by Jacob, makes himself subject to his brother, and leaves the promised land for him to prosper in. This was an incredibly selfless act and an act of true love. Esau models for us that no matter what hurt someone else has caused you, your response is what is important, and your response can allow both of you to prosper. Here's the catch though: that same humble heart has to be without malice as well, as you need to have the desire for the other person to prosper.

How do we develop an attitude like Esau's? How does he get to this place in his life where he runs out to meet the one who betrayed him, kisses his neck and then leaves the land they settle in so that the other one can enjoy it? My only answer is that this only happens when we fix our eyes on Jesus, a man of sorrows who humbled himself on the cross and died for those who wronged and betrayed him.

Genesis 37

One of my favorite books in the Chronicles of Narnia series by C.S. Lewis is *"The Horse and His Boy"*. Truth be told, I read it as an adult for the first time, while I read most of the other books as a child. I doubt I would have liked it much as a child as it doesn't seem to be among the more exciting books in the series, but I loved it as an adult for one paragraph in the book.

I couldn't possibly do it justice here, as describing the book's plot in any detail would take some time. In short, the book is about Shasta, an orphan boy who is found floating in a boat as a young sick child, sold into slavery and through a series of seemingly random circumstances ends up saving the kingdom of Narnia. The events that lead to this seem so unnecessary at best and possibly cruel at worst. The paragraph that means the most to me though, happens when Shasta is lost in the fog at night, and senses that someone is with him. He can't see him, but manages to speak to him as he can sense his presence. Shasta relays his true feelings about the troubles he has gone through, including being pursued by lions twice. He makes the comment, "If nothing else, it was bad luck to meet so many lions." His companion, Aslan, then reveals himself as the single lion whom Shasta has encountered during his journey...

"I was the lion who forced you to join with Aravis. I was the cat who comforted you among the houses of the dead. I was the lion who drove the jackals from you while you slept. I was the lion who gave the horses the new strength of fear for the last mile so that you should reach King Lune in time. And I was the lion you do not remember who pushed the boat in which you lay, a child near death, so that it came to shore where a man sat, wakeful at midnight, to receive you."

C.S. Lewis - The Horse and His Boy

So many things are at play here, but most of all was Aslan's providence. Aslan of course, representing God, has orchestrated every event to prepare young Shasta for the purpose that would be fulfilled in him. The parallels to Joseph's life abound, as the circumstances surrounding his sale to Potiphar seem every bit as random – mere coincidences that lead to one heck of a story in the end.

Was it really a coincidence, though? No, it was a divine plan executed by a divine God. God brought to Jacob's mind the idea to look in on his sons. Perhaps someone in Shechem would have seen what was done to Joseph, so God ordained that brothers would not be there. Someone was in the fields at Shechem though and knew exactly where Joseph's brothers had gone. When he arrived, it was God's will that Reuben was among his brothers when the decision was made to kill him, so that he could talk them into sparing his life. Likewise, God willed that he would not be there when Joseph was sold to the Ishmaelites, as he probably wouldn't have allowed it. The fact that the brothers simply sat by the well and had a snack gave just enough time for the caravan to come by and buy Joseph from them. I'm sure that some bizarre circumstance occurred to facilitate the meetup of the caravan with Potiphar, who bought Joseph and just happened to work for Pharaoh.

In every instance, God was not so much controlling as orchestrating. It was in Reuben's nature to stand up against killing his brother. Judah was always the pragmatist, and the Ishmaelites, being laden with spices and perfumes from far away lands, were always in the market for making a deal. The natural instincts of everyone involved were orchestrated by God to accomplish his purposes. Perhaps even Joseph himself is unscathed here, as he may have been until that point a bit of a loudmouth. Who in their right mind would speak out loud of dreams in which everyone is subject to you and still expect to be perceived of as a good guy? He may have sealed his own fate, but that fate would in turn affect the fate of everyone in the land.

If you're going through some stuff right now, it is appropriate in one sense to ask "why" but not in the sense of "what have a I done to deserve this". Have confidence that God works out everything for the good of those who love him and ask him what you should do. Do that, and while you wait, simply be still, and know that he is God.

Genesis 38

There are times when it seems that the setup for Jesus is almost too perfect. When you consider the prophecies that were fulfilled about him, it seems that he just fits the mold so well. How could anyone ever miss who he is? He MUST be the Messiah!

Indeed, Jesus is the fulfillment of the Old Testament prophecies of the Messiah. From his birthplace, to his escape to Egypt as a child, to his ministry highlights, to the details of his death–it's all there for anyone who wishes to check it out.

Know this though, if we only look at the prophetical trail of Christ, we might miss the historical trail, and that's where some of the best stuff is. That's where you find that the genealogy of Jesus, although perfectly within God's will, is far from ideal. For example, the book of Hebrews speaks about how Jesus was a priest, but not by the law. What that means is that he wasn't from the tribe of Levi. See that? He's not even from the right tribe! Think of who Jesus' ancestors were...David was an adulterer. Ruth wasn't even Jewish to begin with. And then there's Judah–one of the 12 sons of Jacob from whose seed the Messiah would eventually be delivered.

There's not much good to say about the sons of Jacob is there? After Joseph, it's hard to like people who sell others into slavery. None of them are really shown to be the best of men in the Bible.

However, Judah is perhaps given the best treatment. We can at least relate to him on some level. He seems to try to reach for that which is right most of the time. When his brothers decide to kill Joseph, it's Judah who comes up with the alternate plan. When Joseph later asks for Benjamin to come, Judah offers his own life to Jacob if anything happens to Benjamin. When Joseph demands that Benjamin be punished for something he didn't do, it's Judah who pleads his younger brother's case.

Judah certainly has his good moments, and by the time we find him again in chapter 38, he seems to be mostly concerned with what's best for his family. A true patriarch, he realizes that even his daughters-in-law need to be taken care of, and when one of his sons dies, he does his best to make sure that his son's widow won't be alone. Though he tries to pass her off to one of his other sons, two of them die for dishonorable behavior with her. He tells her to go home to her father's house and live as a widow. Later, Judah's own wife dies, and in the midst of his grief, he is deceived by his daughter-in-law into sleeping with her and she conceives.

I have a lot of compassion for Judah. You have to understand what a huge deal this is in that time, and how easily the sin came upon him. He is lonely. He misses his wife. He misses his dead sons. The touch of a woman is so therapeutic to him, and he convinces himself he needs this. After all, he probably thought "I'm not really cheating on anyone anymore". He makes one mistake in the midst of a flood of emotions and ends up paying dearly. He has impregnated his own daughter-in-law and everyone knows about it. You might say, "but he didn't know it was his daughter-in-law" and you'd be right. In fact, before realizing it was his daughter-in-law, Judah simply thought he was going to bed with a prostitute. That's not really the best argument to use if your desire is to allow him to keep the moral high ground on this issue, is it? Indeed, his shame is on full display for all to see.

What I like about the story is simply this: Jesus was perfect, but his ancestors were not. Jesus knew no sin, but was acquainted with every sorrow, every temptation and every pain that we know. I've always known that, but haven't been able to let it's truth soak into me as much as it should. Instead, whenever I give in to temptation, I think about how Jesus would have never done that and then I end up feeling horrible.

In reality, I should take two things from this. First, the purpose of Jesus being sinless was not to show us how to do it, but rather so that he could be offered as a perfect sacrifice for those of us who can't do it. Second, anytime I need further proof, I need to look no further than Judah, who in spite of his sin was chosen as the line to deliver the Messiah to the world.

Judah is a reminder that we are all broken and susceptible to temptation. We all have the ability to throw it all away in an instant, and yet God can still use us in spite of all of that. He's in the business of healing hurts and closing wounds.

Judah must have felt like his influence was no longer valid—that he had no right to speak up anymore. This is the kind of sin that can crush your family for generations, and cause you to cower away in embarrassment. However, by the time Christ arrived on the scene, he would show that Judah's offspring was ready to roar again. He would be the Lion of Judah and would triumph over the sins of his ancestors. John puts it this way in the Book of Revelation...

> "Then I saw in the right hand of him who sat on the throne a scroll with writing on both sides and sealed with seven seals. And I saw a mighty angel proclaiming in a loud voice, "Who is worthy to break the seals and open the scroll?" But no one in heaven or on earth or under the earth could open the scroll or even look inside it. I wept and wept because no one was found who was worthy to open the scroll or look inside. Then one of the elders said to me, "Do not weep! See, the Lion of the tribe of Judah, the Root of David, has triumphed."

Revelation 5:1-5

I look to the story of Judah for inspiration today, and invite you to ask Christ to rewrite your own history into a story of renewal!

Genesis 39

Is there another passage in scripture that so blatantly screams that we ought to work hard at what we do, no matter what our circumstances are? I know, I know...it doesn't seem to work out for Joseph, at least in the short term. After all, Joseph worked in his new master's house as hard as he could and in the end was framed for something he didn't do and thrown in prison.

Whenever something doesn't work out, we tend to link the effort with the result. Our response is "what a waste" or "if I had known how that would have played out, I wouldn't have wasted my time". However, most of time I have found that nothing could be further from the truth—at least upon reflection much later. For example, a couple of times I've had an idea for a business. I decided to give it a try and it didn't work out. I worked incredibly hard at it and during that time I lost my focus on so many things that I cared about. You would think that I would be tempted to call that time a waste, but I know better. If I had not tried it at all, I would have always wondered and this might have kept me from fully selling out to what I'm doing now. If I had tried but not worked so hard, the result would have been the same. I would have always wondered what would have happened had I applied myself. I would have truly felt like a failure. In fact, I would have regretted it.

I was told once that regret should be reserved for things we haven't tried, not things we've done wrong. I would imagine if you could visit Joseph in his prison cell, he'd tell you that he didn't regret a single moment of servitude to Potiphar nor the effort he showed while doing it. If you could allow me to speculate a bit, Joseph's experience in Potiphar's house gave him the education he needed for his next career move, which would be even greater. In Potiphar's house, he had to learn management. He was put in charge of the entire estate. He had to learn all about the different activities that went on, about wages and currency and about communication and leadership. He would not have learned these things had he not applied himself.

No doubt these skills were on display when the prison guard took notice of Joseph. They were the reason he was put in the position that he was in the jail. A small compensation, I'm sure you'll say, but again, it was a stepping stone to what God had for him next. Would Joseph have ended up in Pharaoh's palace if not for the prison guards taking notice of him? In that moment, do you think Joseph regretted the "wasted time" he spent serving in Potiphar's house?

I don't regret failing at things. I regret the times I didn't apply myself. I have come to realize this, **the effort is ours and the results are God's**. We don't question God's results, but we certainly shouldn't feel the right to either if we don't work hard wherever we are. I am reminded of Paul's words to the Colossians...

"And whatever you do, whether in word or deed, do it all in the name of the Lord Jesus, giving thanks to God the Father through him."

Colossians 3:17

Today, honor your King by working hard for your boss, in the home, running your business, doing your school work—whatever you do, do it as if for Him, and trust the he has a plan for you.

Genesis 40

It's not difficult to admire a guy like Joseph. In the midst of some pretty awful circumstances, where his hardship was unjustly thrust upon him as penalty for something he didn't do, he rises above it all and seems to always respond with an amazing attitude. If the world is what we make of it, Joseph was determined to make it different. He does not give a proportional response to his circumstances, as that would almost assuredly be bitterness. Instead, Joseph trades in sorrow for...diligence. I almost said 'joy' there, but let's make sure that we don't go too far, or else we'll expect Joseph to start walking on water as well.

I doubt Joseph was very happy in his circumstances, but I don't think it was a sin not to be either. Sometimes life deals us harsh blows and sometimes we get the really crushing ones. I don't think God expects us to enjoy the experience of either. I can, however, make rational sense of the idea that a person can be so focused on eternity, that hardship becomes more of a detour than it does a roadblock. Indeed, our faith can potentially reach the point that we continue to praise God and serve him with all of our hearts in the midst of the darkest storms of our lives. That's not zealotry, but the natural outflow of a heart fully surrendered to the idea that God is in control and that he will restore us in his time.

I have had some personal struggles where I found myself with nothing to give...or so I thought. When I think of it now, it seems silly, but the fact is that no matter what I had or lacked, my attitude was what made the difference. I am sorry to say that many times, I did not respond very well at all. I would tell myself "if I only had this or that, perhaps I could do something for God". What I failed to do was to faithfully steward what he had given me.

Think about Joseph for a moment. What did he really have? He was in prison, which meant he did not have freedom, family or possessions. The only things that he had were the intangibles: his abilities, his work ethic and his influence.. Sounds like a lot of nothing, right? What good is work ethic in prison? What good is influence if the only people around are the prison guard and your cell mates?

Influence is probably the most poorly used asset in the kingdom of God. It has always been God's plan to use his people's influence on the world in a big way. For this reason, God often put many of his people in high-ranking **serving** positions so that they could affect change. Abraham was in many ways seen as an equal by King Abimilech. Esther became a wife to the king during the Persian empire. Nehemiah was a cup-bearer for the king. And Joseph? Well, at this point, he shares a cell with the recently fired baker and cupbearer for Pharaoh. No, it doesn't seem like much to work with.

The difference between Joseph and the rest of us, is that Joseph seems to understand at a high level that we are meant to use what we **HAVE** and not what we long for. With that in mind, Joseph begins a relationship with the cupbearer. Keep in mind, that his purpose in meeting the cupbearer is not initially catalyzed by his desire to be released from prison, but rather his own compassion...

> *"And one night they both dreamed—the cupbearer and the baker of the king of Egypt, who were confined in the prison— each his own dream, and each dream with its own interpretation. When Joseph came to them in the morning, he saw that they were troubled. So he asked Pharaoh's officers who were with him in custody in his master's house, 'Why are your faces downcast today?'"*
>
> Genesis 40:5-7

Joseph noticed that his new cellmates were sad. God uses every part of our personality to accomplish his purposes, and with Joseph, he used his caring, nurturing side to begin a relationship that would eventually be the impetus that would elevate Joseph to the highest position in Pharaoh's kingdom.

We can learn a lot from Joseph about how to use our influence more, but for now, let's try to get this one thing right–let's look at what we already have and acknowledge that it is more than enough for God to use to do something great. Wouldn't you like to be a part of what he's doing? Surrender involves more than just giving up what we have—it requires us to acknowledge that what we have is all he needs. While you may question whether all God has given you is all he needs, he doesn't and his invitation to you is to allow him to prove it.

Genesis 41

One day God found such favor in his servant, Solomon, that he came to him with an amazing offer. He offered to give to Solomon anything he wanted. He could have all the riches of the earth. He could have rule over all the nations. He could have any woman he wanted. Instead, Solomon asked simply for wisdom, so that he could govern God's people effectively.

I heard a pastor once telling a personal story about how God had used that story in his life. This pastor had been faithful to God for a long time, and felt released to ask God for one thing, the way that Solomon did. He shared how he asked for a loving marriage, and has never regretted it.

Since that time, I've wondered what it would be like if God gave me that opportunity. If God could find me so faithful that I felt released to ask him for one thing, what would I ask for? What would you ask for? Perhaps my answer will change over time, but for the last year, the answer has been the same: **influence**. I would ask God to increase my influence with people. It would be an incredible burden and responsibility to be gifted with great influence, and my fear is that I might squander it. For that reason, part of me doesn't really want it right now, but I want so badly to become the kind of man that would use it exclusively for the glory of God.

It is with this in mind, that I read the account of Joseph's rise to power in Genesis 41. He came through hardship and unjust treatment only to be given an opportunity at greatness in front of Pharaoh himself. Pharaoh asks him to interpret his dreams, which his wisest of counselors could not do. Joseph has one chance to make a good impression and you'd think that he would want to make sure that he looked good in the eyes of Pharaoh. Most of us would see this as an opportunity to feign humility while in reality extolling our own virtues, in order that we could win favor with the King. Perhaps this is where Joseph gives us the best lesson of all: **Always give credit to God**.

"Pharaoh said to Joseph, 'I had a dream, and no one can interpret it. But I have heard it said of you that when you hear a dream you can interpret it.'"

"'I cannot do it,'" Joseph replied to Pharaoh, 'but God will give Pharaoh the answer he desires.'"

Genesis 41:15-16

It was a big risk to be that cheeky with Pharaoh. Knowing the situation, my response might have sounded like "Sure I'll give it a try. Whatcha got?" Joseph's response however is the ideal mix of faith (that without question God would provide the interpretation) and humility (in that Joseph would really just be the messenger).

This story reminds me of how much I have to learn if I want to be trusted with that level of influence. As much as I hate to admit it, I am still full of pride. I hate even writing it, as if it's a secret that no one would have known if I didn't. Pride is the enemy of influence. Let me correct that, Pride is the enemy of **good** influence, as it can only push it's own agenda and has no room for God's plans if they contradict each other. My prayer today scares me so badly that I feel I must write it or I will never honestly ask for it. My prayer, both for me and for you, is that God will do whatever he needs to do to humble us so that we can be emptied of ourselves and filled up with him.

Genesis 42

At the expense of abandoning some of the obvious ongoing themes in Genesis for one day, I can't help but to use the opportunity presented in this chapter to talk about forgiveness.

I have a good friend who has as much a reason as anyone to be unforgiving toward his mother. She was physically and verbally abusive to him all of his life, and since his father passed away, she only seems to call when she needs something from him. I personally led this friend to a relationship with Christ. This was a journey that took two years, and along the way we had to unpack a lot of stuff from his past. At the top of the pile, was the issue with his mother. I remember him asking me once, "what does the Bible say about forgiveness? Do I really have to forgive her for everything she's done to me? Because, I don't know that I'm ready to do that."

Do you have a story like that? Is there someone that you feel convicted about withholding forgiveness from? I know I have before, so my thoughts today are meant to encourage you, as I know what a burden unforgiveness can truly be.

Let's start by answering the question. What does the Bible say about forgiveness? Here are some references that point to basic principles outlined in scripture...

"Be kind to one another, tenderhearted, forgiving one another, as God in Christ forgave you."

Ephesians 4:32

"...as the Lord has forgiven you, so you also must forgive."

Colossians 3:13

"If you do not forgive others their sins, your Father will not forgive your sins."

Matthew 6:15

"Then Peter came up and said to him, 'Lord, how often will my brother sin against me, and I forgive him? As many as seven times?' Jesus said to him, 'I do not say to you seven times, but seventy times seven.'"

Matthew 18:21-22

These verses, and many others like them can be summarized like this: the Bible commands us to forgive others without limits, because God has forgiven us without limit. If you've been wronged by someone, no matter how badly, there is simply no room in scripture for us to withhold forgiveness, as it is a clear statement of our feelings toward how God has forgiven us. For the Christian, forgiveness is a "Pay it Forward" type of concept, and is in fact one of the only areas where we should rightfully feel condemnation for not practicing it. The reason I say this is that the sin of un-forgiveness is not a weakness of the flesh, but rather an unwillingness of the spirit and a hardness of heart.

This brings us back to Joseph, who in this chapter comes face-to-face with his brothers who ruined his life years earlier because of their jealousy. Let's be honest, what they did to him was probably worst than anything that's been done to most of us. Surely if anyone had reason to withhold forgiveness it was Joseph.

Of course, Joseph does forgive his brothers in the end, but not without a little bit of drama as a prelude. You might think that Joseph's actions are not forgiving at first, and that perhaps he was struggling with finding room in his heart to overlook the offenses committed against him. However, I see something more nuanced than that.

As a pastor, it always feels slightly irresponsible to present anything in the Bible as nuanced. We have such a built-in reverence for black and white authority and Scripture is certainly that. However, when we discuss forgiveness, we ought not to do so without admitting that wisdom has it's place in reconciliation as well. What I mean to say is that I believe there is a difference between forgiveness and offering someone a second chance. Certainly there are times when forgiveness is accompanied by second chances, but they aren't inextricably linked.

For example, let's imagine a couple with two kids. The husband is physically and verbally abusive to both the wife and the kids. He always feels bad later and apologizes, but eventually goes back to his old ways. One day one of the kids winds up seriously injured and the wife finally has had enough. She leaves him for the safety of her children as much as her own. Some time later, the husband turns his life around. Actually, let's go one step further and say that the husband finds Christ and significantly turns his life around. He comes back to his wife and in the most sincere way possible, humbly apologizes for his behavior and tearfully asks for her forgiveness.

Now, if the wife is a believer, I would suggest that she needs to forgive the husband, as she is certainly not perfect herself and has been forgiven of much by God. However, I still grant her the right to decide whether or not it is a good idea to reconcile fully and immediately place him back in the home, or even in the lives of her children based on the circumstances. She could be putting her children at risk, and it may be more appropriate to forgive the past, with some wise caution being reserved for the future.

What we see here with Joseph is a bit of a test. I believe that more than anything Joseph wants to reconcile. However, the level to which they will be able to reconcile will greatly depend on if his brothers have changed their ways. If he takes the lid off and reveals who he truly is then his brothers may act differently out of fear. He wants to know how they act when he's not in the room. Make sense?

It's a fine line to walk as this kind of discernment can easily manifest itself inappropriately. If we approach possible reconciliation with "I'll forgive you but I'll never forget" or "let's put you on trial to see how you do" then we won't have a chance. On the other hand, I also believe that unless biblical forgiveness allows for this type of discernment, there may be some people that we never even try to forgive as there is simply to much risk involved.

Let me be clear that I believe we need more forgiveness, not less. We need to take chances on relationships that have been broken and need to be restored. The slate isn't wiped clean in the sense that we forget what they're capable of, but rather we no longer bring up their past offenses. This is the type of forgiveness that Joseph offers—one that is willing to forgive people of the worst kind of injustice, while being tempered by a wisdom that comes from experience.

With all of that said, I hope it wasn't too pragmatic to be personally challenging. We need to be challenged in this area. So here it is: Who is it that you need to forgive? Isn't it time that you laid that burden down? Hasn't it ruined your life enough? When we refuse to forgive, we are the ones who suffer, not the people who wronged us. We carry that chip on our shoulder. We get furious at the sight of the person and loathe any success they have. We allow their misdeeds to ruin our ability to enjoy life on any given day while we fixate on their awfulness. When this happens, not only have they hurt us in the past, but now we allow them to continually hurt us in the future. Let's turn the tables and allow their misdeeds to give us something positive–a

personal experience of something beautiful, of forgiving the way
we ourselves have been forgiven.

Genesis 43

Picking up where we left off in the last chapter, I thought I would share some thoughts about reconciliation in a more practical way.

If you have identified a broken relationship in your life I hope that it would be your desire to reconcile. If so, perhaps you're wondering how to go about doing it? Of course, apologies need to be made and perhaps you've done that. Maybe you've smiled and greeted each other warmly at church or the supermarket. Now what? What can you do to bring the reconciliation to some type of crescendo?

I would suggest to you that there is something that you can do that will honor the individual and give you opportunity for extended fellowship: invite them to a meal in your home.

This is a lost art in my generation. We seem to have forgotten how to respect this time-honored tradition. For millenniums, a meal at someone's home was a real event for everyone involved. The best food was made, the best dishes were used and the scope of the evening went far longer than an hour. This is especially true of Jewish culture, but most cultures revere having someone into their home as a way of showing them great servitude. Is there a better place for reconciliation to happen, than over a meal that you have personally prepared and now serve to your guests?

Is there a better way to show someone that you are serious about your relationship?

This can have an enormous impact on someone. Imagine a relationship where you hurt someone. Imagine you said something really cutting, and ripped their life apart with your words. You've felt guilty ever since, and have lost countless nights of sleep over it. How do you recover from that? Even after apologies are made, and you are once again cordial with each other, what can restore that type of relationship?

With the caveat that it may never be the same again, imagine the impact it would have on you if that person then invited you to their home for a meal. Their actions speak louder than their words. They may have accepted your apology months ago, but this...they're inviting you to come into their home, to be around their kids and to spend an evening together with you in conversation. What an immense gesture that would be.

We've lost the art of entertaining. I will admit that most times I would prefer to go out to eat with others, and this is purely a pragmatic choice. I have children and sometimes they act up, so by going out to eat, I can choose the time of our departure more easily. Spending time in a home doesn't leave that option. It demands a looser schedule, and a lengthier conversation. This can only be good for us, as it causes us to reach beyond what we're comfortable with and that's a great way to get to intimacy in a relationship.

As Joseph moves toward reconciliation with his brothers in Genesis 43, we can only speculate about what he's waiting for. Perhaps he's still working through his anger, and perhaps he just doesn't trust them. Whatever the case might be, he tries to overcome his apprehension and decides to take a step of faith and invite them into his home for a meal. At this meal, they ate their fill and drank far into the night. In this atmosphere, everyone just enjoyed each other's company and this was most likely the catalyst for Joseph to make amends as the goodness of their current fellowship far outweighed the hurt of the past.

Jesus spent a lot of his time at a table in someone's home. When he told Zacchaeus he would come to his home, you can bet that a meal was served. Before entering Jerusalem for his last week, he had a deeply spiritual moment over a meal at Simon's house with Lazarus, Mary and Martha. His last night on earth centered around a special meal with his disciples. He chose a breakfast of fish and chips to have a "come to Jesus" meeting with Peter. Jesus never missed an opportunity to deepen his relationships and further his influence over a meal in someone's home.

Who can you invite to your home this week? What relationship do you have that could use that sort of act of kindness? Figure it out and extend the invitation. Then, spend a few days getting ready and really put on a show if you can. Honor them in your home and serve them well. Your faith will deepen, your character will grow and their heart will soften. Most importantly, God will be honored and you will have the opportunity to praise him for what he has done.

Genesis 44

I'd like to start today with a bit of an aside note about where we are and where we've come from. The events that occur between Joseph and his brothers are unfolding slowly. For me, attempting to glean some message of inspiration from each chapter feels like I'm trying to squeeze water out of a handful of desert sand. Sometimes that's how it is with God's Word. Sometimes, the text is simply less "spiritual" or at the very least, less interesting as is the case with some of the genealogies that we've been through. Sometimes, if we're honest, the problem is with us as we have other things on our mind or we're just not that into it.

This, above anything else for me, is the point of this book and this journey through Genesis. It is an attempt to show practically that God's Word never returns void, and that Paul was right when he wrote to Timothy that "all scripture is God-breathed and is profitable (2 Tim. 3:16)". Sometimes we have to reach for it, as I will be doing with this chapter, but that's not really a bad thing, is it? If I work hard at trying to get something out of scripture, it will at the very least signal that I WANT to get something out of it and that I BELIEVE something is there and that's certainly an appropriate attitude to have when studying God's Word.

So here we go.

I believe that Joseph is still holding out because he is waiting for that one moment that will just grip his heart to forgive his brothers. He has given them plenty of opportunities and they seem to be showing good character. They haven't lied to him. They've done what he's asked. When they find silver in their sacks, they go back to him and apologize. They bow down before him in humility. What is he waiting for? I think he's still torn. He wants to go there...to forgive his brothers, but he's dwelled on the hurt they caused him for so long that it's become a cancer in his very soul. Something inside is holding him back like a dam blocking a river's flow. Whatever capacity he has for love, it has been contained behind this immovable obstacle.

As a pastor, I've been able to witness firsthand lives being changed by the power of Christ. I've seen hearts of stone melt like butter from the warmth of the gospel message. If there is one thing that these experiences have taught me it's that we're all the same in this regard: we all respond powerfully to a message of self-sacrifice. Nothing impacts the emotions of the human spirit more than witnessing someone offering to take punishment or hardship in the place of someone else so that they won't have to. It is a story that has been idealized in legends and revered in films like Titanic, Saving Private Ryan, Star Wars, The Matrix and Independence Day, among others. It's no coincidence that the characters who die in place of others—John Clark in "The Green Mile" and John Creasy in "Man on Fire" have the initials "J.C.". It's in our nature...we are predisposed to respond to a message of sacrifice, like the message of the cross. Jesus said it this way...

"Greater love has no one than this: to lay down one's life for one's friends."

John 15:13

So what it is that finally breaks the dam in Joseph's heart and allows for his emotion to come pouring out like a flood? It's listening to his brother Judah, begging to be imprisoned in place of his younger brother, Benjamin. Whatever hatred for his brothers might have been rooted in Joseph's heart, the impact of Judah's act was simply too great, and that hatred was washed away by an overwhelming river of love.

I love that. Joseph's heart was moved in many ways by the same emotion that has drawn all believers to the gospel message. It's an emotion only felt by someone who has experienced someone dying for them, being sacrificed in their place. I have experienced that first hand and the love I feel as a result is enough to allow me to forgive thousands of wrongs against me. Thank you, Lord, for taking my place. May I always respond to that act by forgiving others and loving them in spite of what they might have done to me.

Genesis 45

In this chapter we find Joseph finally making peace with his brothers. It is a terribly emotional scene, full of tears and embraces. Verse 15 tells us that after Joseph reveals who he is and spends time kissing them and weeping with them, his brothers "talked with him awhile". I'm sure that was a long conversation, full of admissions of guilt, repentance and the acknowledgment that it has been way too long. Finally, when the baggage is completely unpacked, they become brothers again and there's a lot of catching up to do. Joseph hears about the wives, sons and daughters of each one, about who is the better farmer or hunter, and what the old town looks like today. It is a joyous occasion and one that wouldn't be possible without the power of forgiveness.

I have to admit as I read this that it became more real to me than ever before. Of course, as we get older and grow in knowledge of God's Word, different passages that we haven't read in some time take on a whole new life. Perhaps for me, it is simply because I have brothers who live far away and every time we get together it is a joyous occasion. We truly celebrate what it means to be husbands and fathers and what it takes to lead in our homes. We affirm each other's success and admire how each other has grown. All of these emotions are so accessible in this story and I can only imagine how Joseph has longed for this moment...how he has dreamed about it, and how he probably never thought it would ever be possible.

Amidst all of this, I see something that is speaking to me as a leader. While I do believe that we can't put leaders up on pedestals, I believe that leaders have to hold themselves accountable. We simply have to be the ones to step out in faith first. The way I see Joseph doing this is in how he forgives his brothers. What he essentially says is, "thank you for your apology, but please don't lose anymore sleep over it. Rather, join me in celebrating because it is obvious that this was a part of God's plan to bless all of us in a time of great hardship."

Now, I don't know if he actually felt like that. I'm inclined to believe that he could have and probably did still have some very real hurt deep inside that was always in danger of bubbling to the surface. However, realizing the great influence inherent in his position, he must have recognized that in order to get beyond it, someone was going to have to make a gesture toward the other. A great gulf, caused by his brother's actions, still existed between them, and the one who was offended (Joseph) realized that the only chance of true reconciliation with them was for him to step into that space and bridge the gap.

The connection to what Christ did for us in reconciling himself to us is obvious, but perhaps not so obvious is the leadership that is shown in Joseph. It may seem like I'm grasping at straws, but I can't get over this one verse...

"Then he sent his brothers away, and as they departed, he said to them, 'Do not quarrel on the way.'"

Genesis 45:24

I find that to be so amazing because in the midst of an episode where Joseph could have excused himself from the responsibility of fixing everybody's lives for one day, he recognizes something in his brothers: they still fight all the time. They still argue and it disrupts their unity. Joseph, recognizing this, realizes that in that moment, he needs to use his new-found influence with them to help them. In fact, I would suggest that a part of the reason for his forgiveness is so that he can earn the right to speak into their lives. By removing the barrier between them, he earns enough leverage to be able to help them with a problem that has gone on for too long. In this moment, Joseph quickly moves from the position of martyr to that of a spiritual father because he is a leader, and leaders always step up. When the going gets tough, leaders always stand in the gap.

I am in awe of this man and am challenged by his behavior. What grace must have been afforded to him and what humility must be in his possession. If I am to ever imagine playing on that kind of level, I have to fully internalize one very central idea: it's not about me. Guess what? It's not about you. It's about God and his glory and we have a part to play in that. Whether you're a leader or not, God is looking for people to stand in the gap. It's how healing happens. Jesus modeled it on the cross and said...

"Whoever wants to be my disciple must deny themselves and take up their cross and follow me."

Matthew 16:24

In short, it's what followers of Christ do. Freely we have received, and freely we give. Freely we forgive, because freely we have been forgiven.

Genesis 46

I remember sitting at my kitchen table when my wife and I signed up for life insurance. A nice gentleman who came recommended by a friend sat across from us and walked us through everything. It was a good thing to do, and I don't regret providing that sort of security for my family in the event of tragedy. However, I've sat through a couple of those types of sales pitches and I can't get over how cavalier a salesman can be when suggesting the death of someone. Truly, a tactic that must be a pre-requisite taught by every insurance firm is to at some point in the conversation say something like "if something happens to you, you don't want your wife to be going through the red tape, you want me to come to your door and hand your wife a big check."

For some reason this part always catches me off-guard. I guess it's because I've recognized that they all seem to not-so-subtly glorify the potential "largeness" of that check. They never talk about just handing over a check. They talk about handing over a (insert your favorite "large-sized" adjective here) check. Is that supposed to impress me? Am I really supposed to start thinking about the possibilities or even opportunities that could be afforded my family as a consolation for my passing?

As I'm still young, healthy and have people who love me, I don't enjoy the thought of dying. I too quickly dismiss Paul's arguments in Philippians 1 for why he longs for death as the mere ramblings of one who doesn't have a family. I don't share his ideas of "it's better for them if I stick around". It is of course, but I want to experience their future here on earth as well. I suppose it really comes down to the fact that I'm so naive about the awesomeness of eternity with God that I just don't know any better.

It is for these reasons that I simply can't empathize or even sympathize with an old person's desire to "die in peace". Jacob makes reference to it twice here. In fact, he even dreams about it...

"And God spoke to Israel in visions of the night and said, 'Jacob, Jacob.' And he said, 'Here I am.' Then he said, 'I am God, the God of your father. Do not be afraid to go down to Egypt, for there I will make you into a great nation. I myself will go down with you to Egypt, and I will also bring you up again, and Joseph's hand shall close your eyes.'"

Genesis 46:2-4

The idea that this motivates Jacob to get a move on more than suggests that he wants to depart from this life, but doesn't feel he can go in peace unless he sees for himself that Joseph lives. To a point, this emotion is echoed in the life of Simeon who desired to see the Messiah before he died. Later on, when Jacob does finally meets Joseph, some of the first words out of his mouth are "now that I know you're alive, let me die."

I doubt I'll understand these words for a while, but I have watched others who could. I've watched friends die of cancer in the most undignified fashion. I have heard of poverty so great that it makes me question whether or not the children would have been better off if they hadn't been born. I know this world is broken and for some, no amount of familial love will ever outweigh the hardship of their lives. In these times, I marvel at the words that the apostle Paul quoted from the book of Isaiah...

> *"What no eye has seen, nor ear heard, nor the heart of man imagined, what God has prepared for those who love him."*
>
> 1 Corinthians 2:9

I trust this to mean that I haven't seen it because my eyes couldn't even take it in. I haven't heard it because there are waves of sound too beautiful for my ears. Of course, I couldn't imagine it because my heart couldn't contain the love that must be evident in the creation of heaven. I believe the sight alone would overwhelm a heart that truly understands that God made it for them.

I once read that the best thing a Christian could do to keep his heart set on God is to meditate about the reality of heaven for a half-hour every day. This kind of focus puts everything into that

"Kingdom" perspective that we as Christians are so quick to admonish each other with.

I don't want to die, but I want to be desperate for what awaits me on the other side. While others are searching for something that makes life worth living, I am searching for that which makes this life worth leaving.

Genesis 47

There is an interesting story of social welfare that is told in Genesis 47. As the famine continues to rage on for years in the land of Egypt, everyone comes to Joseph for help.

One year when they come pleading for food, their argument is that they have no money left. Joseph's response is that they should exchange their livestock for food, which they do and their families are fed.

The next year, having no livestock, they come to Joseph and ask again. **This time**, they have an idea of their own. They will offer to Joseph the only thing that they have left...their land.

You might think, "How enraged they must feel about Joseph!" The idea that we would come to one of our leaders and say to them "I have no food, please help" and their response is "what are you going to give me in return" sounds reprehensible to us.

In our country we like to believe that the little guy has a chance. That's good. I think the attitude of picking ourselves up by our bootstraps is what has made America great today. However, it is simply not how the Bible describes a great society. For many of us, the Bible challenges us in a way that makes us uncomfortable when it comes to how a society or an economy should be run.

What we find in the Old Testament is that in the most revered societies—such as the one that Joseph was in charge of—there is no redistribution of wealth. There are the "haves" and the "have nots". The best case scenario is that the "haves" recognize their responsibility to the "have nots" and work out an arrangement to provide for them. If in that provision their wealth increases (such is the case with Joseph in this chapter), it is taken with the purpose of enhancing the government's ability to provide for the people.

Now, I am not going to waste a whole chapter of God's word talking about politics. Rather, I gave that background so that I could put the response of the people in the proper context.

When the people come to Joseph the first time and Joseph asks for their livestock in exchange for food, I'm sure they weren't expecting that. I'm sure they didn't know what to expect. What I find interesting is how they respond to the offer. Obviously they accept it, but we find that they consider it appropriate on some level. Perhaps this response was formed over time as they considered their plight, but nevertheless, when they come the next year, they are so convinced of it's validity that they approach Joseph with an attitude of humble gratitude and even servitude.

Their thought process must have been that "we wouldn't have any food if not for this man. Therefore, we owe him our lives in service." So they come to him with their requests and in exchange offer to become his servants.

I wonder if we approach God in the same way. I wonder if we feel the need to. When we come to God in prayer, do we feel entitled to his blessing because we're so focused on how much he loves us that we just feel it's what he wants to do anyway? After all, when you love someone, you want to give them everything, right? God loves me, therefore he wants to give me everything and I should let him, right?

We're so focused on his love for us that we often forget how much we don't deserve it. Make no mistake—We don't deserve it. To truly appreciate that, you'd have to live in a society where you actually felt like the wealthy people deserved to have all the money and you don't. Let's face facts, **God has everything and is entitled to it**.

The point of all of this is not that God requires anything from us. He doesn't. The point is that the people, in spite of the fact that they had nothing left to offer, found a way to offer something to Joseph...that of their entire lives in service to him.

The question is simple. When you approach the throne of God today, what do you have to offer him?

Genesis 48

I used to attend a church that played a lot of what I'd call "gospel" music. These songs were backed by a great band. Good drums, a bass guitar thumping out a beat, a piano, an electric guitar and of course, an organ, which was played amazingly by the pastor's wife. One of my favorite songs to sing there was "The Enemy's Camp". The main lyrics of the song were "I went to the enemy's camp and I took back what he stole from me."

The song is a reference to a story found in 1 Samuel 30, where the city of Ziklag is attacked and plundered by the Amalekites. David was marching a small army of his men to the city, but was too late to stop the attack. The Amalekites carried off all the women and children as well as many valuables from the city. David asks God whether or not he should pursue the Amalekites, given the fact that he is incredibly outnumbered and they are surely some distance away by now and his men haven't eaten. God affirms to David that he should pursue them, which he then does. He defeats everyone of them and brings back the spoils. Not one Amalekite got away and every single soul was brought back to the city.

The story is an epic one no doubt, but the impact of the song has been far greater for me. Others might wax eloquent on the means by which David received his instruction or the generosity he shows in the end in the sharing of the spoils. For me, however, it's all about the idea behind the song: when the enemy takes something from us, we redeem it. We don't just move on. We reclaim it for the kingdom.

This thought has different applications for many people. I've certainly used it in music. I grew up in really traditional, fundamental circles. These were the kind of churches and institutions that would chastise the kind of music that I would listen to. I remember one message in particular in Bible school talking about the "noise of war" that was in the camp when Moses descended from Mount Sinai, and how this noise was akin to today's contemporary Christian music.

This same thought existed when we first planted Lakeside Church and the point was brought up that our music shouldn't sound like the world's music. My rebuttal to that was that it's the other way around. I believe all music belongs to God. No poet is more inspired than the one who sings about the ultimate lover and the ultimate creator in God. I believe in this regard that we are to take back God's music from the world. We are to reclaim it for his glory. I would suggest that almost anything bad can be redeemed by man to be used for the glory of God.

If you're wondering what this has to do with the story of Joseph, it was been inspired by Jacob's last words to Joseph...

"I have given to you rather than to your brothers one mountain slope that I took from the hand of the Amorites."

Genesis 48:22

In other versions you might read that Joseph was given a "ridge" or a "portion" of land, but it was not so unspecified. In fact, the actual word that is used is "shekem" or "shechem". This was the very land where Levi and Simeon tricked the men of the city into circumcising themselves and then attacked and killed them all in retribution for the rape of their sister, Dinah. Jacob was furious at them for this. It was wrong, and now he owned a piece of land that was attained in a sinful manner. This plagued Jacob for the rest of his life. However, he makes it right in the end by giving it to Joseph. He sees in Joseph a Godly man–one who will bring honor to what has been dishonorable for so long. He gives the land to Joseph, and in doing so, challenges him to reclaim for God what has been tainted by sin.

It would be difficult for me to give a general statement of practical advice on this. It's much easier to speak of it anecdotally, but in the interest of trying, I would say that when we so readily avoid the things that have a bad history, we miss out on the opportunity to see God redeem it. Furthermore, if we are more than conquerors, why are we so afraid to engage the enemy? Why would we not in boldness stand in the face of what the enemy has taken and declare "it is no longer yours!"?

Remember Braveheart? I love when William Wallace attacks a specific English outpost and allows for a few to survive to bring a message back to the enemy...

> *"Go back to England, and tell them there that Scotland's daughters and her sons are yours no more."*
>
> **William Wallace**

Perhaps the hardest part is identifying what the enemy has taken, so let's start with the easy (as in easy to identify) stuff. Whatever the enemy has taken from you personally—your joy, your self-worth, your courage, your power, your identity, etc— reclaim it today. Tell the enemy that your life is his no more. Reclaim it for the glory of God and experience the power of redemption!

Genesis 49

If you were laying on your death-bed, what would be your final words to your family? Would you use the time to simply tell them how much you love each of them? Would you apologize for any hurt you might have caused in the past? I suppose in the end, your message might be different for each of them. For Jacob, while his life was cut short, he had a lengthy time of 17 years or more to say goodbye. Perhaps whatever emotion he may have had was replaced by a sense of urgency because all Jacob could think about is the future. During Jacob's last few moments on earth, he gives a sort of prophecy for each of his sons. We don't know if he knew the information beforehand and was waiting for the right moment, but we do know that he accurately predicted the future for all 12 men. Some futures were brilliant and glorious and others not so much. However, one stands out for me above all the rest...Judah.

"Judah, your brothers will praise you;
your hand will be on the neck of your enemies;
your father's sons will bow down to you.
You are a lion's cub, Judah;
you return from the prey, my son.
Like a lion he crouches and lies down,
like a lioness—who dares to rouse him?
The scepter will not depart from Judah,

nor the ruler's staff from between his feet,

until he to whom it belongs shall come

and the obedience of the nations shall be his."

Genesis 49:8-10

Out of Judah would spring a mighty nation. King David would come from his seed. This is what is meant by "your brothers will praise you" and "your father's sons will bow down to you". In fact, it would mean that their tribes would be united under his banner when David became King. King David would be mighty in battle as well, and his victories would be celebrated and sung for generations. Of course this kingdom, as mighty as it is, would pale in comparison with the king "to whom it belongs shall come".

Because of this prophecy, the symbol for the tribe of Judah became a lion. Not as a lion who is enraged, but as one who is aware of his power and authority and therefore lies down without fear. The great theologian Matthew Henry wrote this about these verses...

*"The lion is the king of beasts, the terror of the forest when he roars; when he seizes his prey, none can resist him; when he goes up from the prey, none dare pursue him to revenge it. By this it is foretold that the tribe of Judah should become very formidable, and should not only obtain great victories, but should **peaceably and quietly enjoy what was obtained by***

*those victories—that they should make war, not for the sake of war, but **for the sake of peace**. Judah is compared, not to a lion rampant, always tearing, always raging, always ranging; but to a lion couchant, enjoying the satisfaction of his power and success, without creating vexation to others: **this is to be truly great**."*

Matthew Henry

Of course, this passage is also very prophetic. It's not about Judah, but about his seed. Even though his time would not come for over a thousand years, this passage is referring to the Messiah. This is why Micah writes about his origins...

"But you, Bethlehem Ephrathah, though you are small among the clans of Judah, out of you will come for me one who will be ruler over Israel, whose origins are from of old, from ancient times."

Micah 5:2

Not only did the Messiah come from the tribe of Judah, but Jesus was given the title that had become symbolic of the tribe. As John beheld the throne of God, he saw a scroll in his right hand, and an angel asked who was worthy to open it. No one was found worthy, and John wept, until one of the elders pointed him to Jesus...

"Then one of the elders said to me, 'Do not weep! See, the Lion of the tribe of Judah, the Root of David, has triumphed. He is able to open the scroll and its seven seals.'"

Revelation 5:5

What I love most about this title given to Jesus is which two books it is referenced in. The entire Bible is a collection of 66 books, but in many ways it has always been destined to be one volume and that has never been more apparent than here. The entire volume points to one person—Jesus, the Lion of Judah— and his title, which found it's origins in the first book of the Bible (Genesis), was fulfilled and given in the last book (Revelation). Like bookends to a great story, Jesus is presented as this mighty lion, who is destined to bring peace into the world.

Genesis 50

If I can share personally here at the end of our journey through Genesis, I have been amazed at the roller-coaster of emotion I have been through during this time. It was only 50 days, and yet God dealt with me personally in many ways. He challenged my faith and helped me see that I need to step out more and meet him where he is—again, not in terms of effort, but in terms of faith. He challenged my convictions and made me realize that I've compromised in areas of my life that have affected my character. More than anything though, I have been pointed to his Son Jesus, and my faith in the fact that God's plan was to offer his son as a sacrifice for me has grown immeasurably.

In this last chapter, I see Joseph being a sort of type of Christ, however subtly, in his final response to his brother's treatment of him years before. Jacob, his father, has just died and his brother's are naturally worried that Joseph's wrath would finally be made known now that his father is not alive to temper his actions. They make up a lie about Jacob's last wish being that Joseph would forgive his brothers. Joseph sees right through it, but speaks kindly to them, letting them know that he came to terms with it long ago...

"But Joseph said to them, 'Don't be afraid. Am I in the place of God? You intended to harm me, but God intended it for good to accomplish what is now being done, the saving of many lives.'"

Genesis 50:19-20

Wow, what a response. There are certainly times when we are called to have that kind of perspective about things that happen to us. When tough times come, we inevitably receive a word of encouragement from a Christian brother or sister that reminds us what the apostle Paul wrote in his letter to the Rome...

"And we know that God causes everything to work together for the good of those who love God and are called according to his purpose for them."

Romans 8:28

I believe that the words above are true, and I've seen it play out in my own life. I will go through a trial questioning God as to why it's happening only to come out on the other side and understand that he had a plan for my good all along. However, in Joseph's case this verse takes on a very different meaning for me. You see, typically we think of the meaning of this verse to be that God sometimes takes us through valleys in order to bring us to another mountaintop. He allows us to suffer so that we can eventually prosper. What this suggests though is that we expect God to use our suffering in our own lives. Sometimes, though, he might allow for someone to suffer so that someone else can receive the blessing. This is a little harder to swallow as it hardly seems fair, but some of God's best servants have experienced this first-hand.

While Joseph was eventually elevated to power as a result of his suffering, he acknowledged that God allowed him to go through it for his family's benefit. God used the event to allow the leaders of the 12 tribes of Jacob to prosper after the famine. In fact the whole nation would be saved, prompting Joseph to view his suffering as necessary to save the lives of many. This makes Joseph like Christ in a way because Christ himself was known as the "suffering servant." His blood was poured out for all people and his life was offered as a ransom for many. The famous passage written by the prophet Isaiah explains it this way...

*"And because of his experience,
my righteous servant will make it possible
for many to be counted righteous,
for he will bear all their sins."*

Isaiah 53:11

How does this challenge me? If I am ever called to suffer for the sake of other people and not just myself, I pray that God will find me faithful and that I will be willing to use my life for him in this way. I worry that I might not feel the same way when I'm actually in it, but I know it would be a tremendous honor, and one that is undeserved...to have the opportunity to imitate my Savior in this way.

Your Turn

I want to thank you, the reader, for allowing me to share my personal journey through Genesis with you. This book is in many ways an altar...a commemorative item that symbolizes a journey that God has taken me through. I literally set aside 50 days for this project, reading and reflecting on a chapter each day. At times it was a grind, but having that sort of disciplined process reaped a great harvest for me in the end. Now, I'd like to challenge you to fully experience God in the current season of your life.

Years ago I discovered how valuable the practice of journaling could really be. Sadly, it's not a discipline that I've been able to maintain as much as I want, but the ability to look back and read a few short thoughts about my experience a year ago...thoughts that seemed so incredibly ordinary at the time now have such great meaning for me.

So how do you do it effectively? My best wisdom in this area after years of various successes and failures is to take 5 minutes every night and follow the process I've outlined below. Again, do it at night, right before bed when it's quiet because it's typically easier to form the habit at the end of the day than at the start. Also, you'll be able to reflect on your day. Try to not allow yourself to take too long at it. 5 minutes is more than enough. During that 5 minutes, do these 3 things...

Reflect

Get a notebook, put the date at the top of a page and write a couple of short sentences about your day. It doesn't have to be long at all, but try to include either how you feel (either physically, emotionally or spiritually), what questions, concerns or fears you have, and any important interactions you may or may not have had that day. Try to avoid only writing about what you think is significant...you may be surprised at the significance of insignificant things later on. Keep it short and sweet...a minute or two at most.

Read

Read one chapter from God's Word. Don't put too much pressure on yourself to understand it—most of us aren't Bible scholars, we'll have more questions than answers most of the time, and that's okay, as we'll show in the next step. Have trouble focusing when you're reading? Guess what? Me too. No condemnation here. The goal here, especially when you're trying to form habits is just that...to form the habit. That comes from quantity not quality. The important thing is how often you're doing it not how much you're getting out of it.

Respond

It's important that you respond in some way to what God has said. My best advice is to do one of three things: 1) Ask a question about what you've read, 2) write down a favorite verse in the chapter, or 3) take a shot at what the passage is saying to you that night. Make sure it is relevant to what you're going through though. This isn't a time for coming up with teaching for others. Make it personal.

Again, no pressure here...you should see my journals! Sometimes I write a couple of paragraphs, but sometimes I end up writing something like this: *"this seems like a really interesting story to me...I'm so tired right now, but I'd love to learn more about who Samson was sometime."* In fact, most of the time, it's as short as the latter, but I allow for that because the habit is more important than the product.

Request

God LOVES it when his people pray! I know a few of you struggle with this part of your life as I have, so let me encourage you to do this: write out a prayer that is one to two sentences in your journal each day. It might be something like this: *"God, when the enemy is attacking me tomorrow, please give me the strength to overcome him."* Whatever it is, write it down and pray it sincerely from your heart.

You may wonder what the point of all of this is when it seems like so little, but I can tell you from experience that when you make it personal like this, you'd be amazed when you look back months later how much you've forgotten about what you went through. You still remember the events, but not necessarily the daily emotion of it all. Even the times I simply wrote down a question...often I've found the answer later and forgot that I asked the question! A journal, in the end, is a record of God working in your life. Then, whenever you're going through a tough season, you have written proof from your own hand that God is always there and always has a plan for you—even when you can't see it at the time.

So that's it. Simply take a 5 minutes just before bed and develop these habits. Here they are again...

- **Reflect** on your day in a journal

- **Read** one chapter in the Bible.

- **Respond** to your reading in some way.

- **Request** God's power in your life.

My prayer is that you would discover this for yourself and I'd love to hear about it if it has made a difference for you! May God's power and grace pour out of your life as you reflect on your journey with Him!

Thanks for reading! If you'd like to read more, visit me on my personal blog and website at www.mattjones.ca.

www.ingramcontent.com/pod-product-compliance
Lightning Source LLC
LaVergne TN
LVHW091216080426
835509LV00009B/1019